DEDICATED TO

*The miners, prospectors
and settlers,
who in their search for wealth and riches,
have in turn given
riches back to the state...*

Thompson's Dry Diggin's in the first weeks after the gold discovery in March, 1851. The man on the left leaning on the shovel is Abraham Thompson, the discoverer of gold in Yreka. The site is now marked with a bronze plaque and is located on the western slopes of Yreka.

Where to Find GOLD in Northern California

James Klein

Gem Guides Book Company

Library of Congress Catalog Card No. 99-73309
ISBN 1-889786-05-5

Cover Design by Bruce Barton
Maps by Jean Hammond

Published by
GEM GUIDES BOOK COMPANY
315 Cloverleaf Drive, Suite F
Baldwin Park, CA 91706

Manufactured in the United States of America

CONTENTS

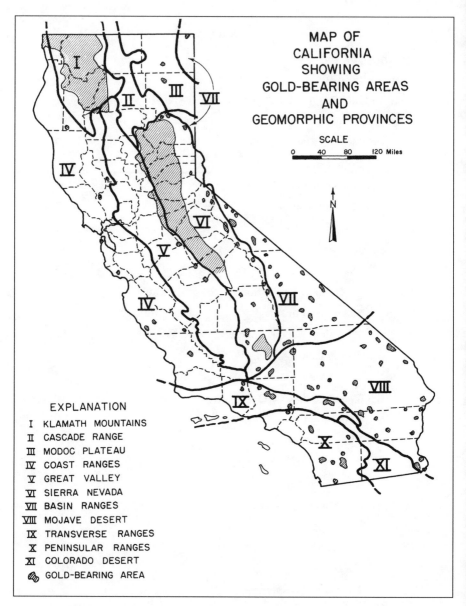

MAP OF
CALIFORNIA
SHOWING
GOLD-BEARING AREAS
AND
GEOMORPHIC PROVINCES

SCALE

0   40   80   120 Miles

N

EXPLANATION

I   KLAMATH MOUNTAINS
II CASCADE RANGE
III MODOC PLATEAU
IV COAST RANGES
V   GREAT VALLEY
VI SIERRA NEVADA
VII BASIN RANGES
VIII MOJAVE DESERT
IX TRANSVERSE RANGES
X   PENINSULAR RANGES
XI COLORADO DESERT
    GOLD-BEARING AREA

(Reprinted by permission, from California Division of Mines and Geology, *Gold Districts of California*, 12)

INTRODUCTION

Northwestern California gets cheated of its importance in gold mining history. It was as much a part of the Gold Rush as the Mother Lode country. Miners rushed to this area just as they did to the Sierra Nevada and found lots of gold in its rivers and creeks and even along its beaches. You can still find gold here today. You will find that the areas here are not worked as much as places near large populations, which increases your chance of making some good finds. It is some of the most beautiful country you will ever see. I love the area and hope you will too. Like a lot of areas in California it owes most of its development to gold mining. After the miners moved out they left the ghost towns behind. What's left now is a pleasant combination of old and new. Everything is here if you just want to pan a little gold or drop a six- or eight-inch dredge in the water. There are lots of nice campgrounds near most all the mining areas to set up a base camp. It is well worth the time and effort to visit the region for a day or two, or stay forever if you want. Take plenty of warm clothes as the nights can get chilly most of the year but the days are always beautiful. I hope to see you out there . . .

Jim Klein

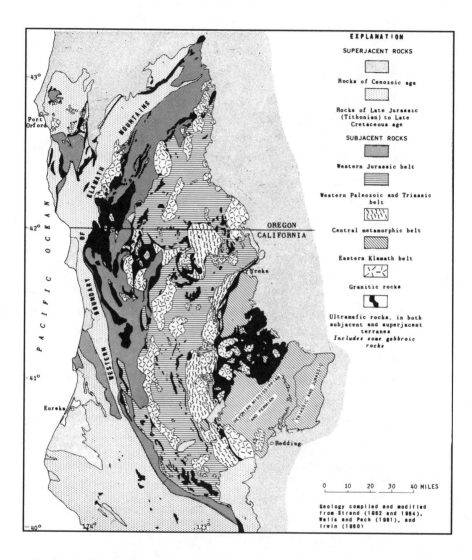

Geological map of Northwestern California and Southwestern Oregon.
(Reprinted by permission, from California Division of Mines and Geology,
Geology of Northern California, 22)

1. GEOLOGY OF NORTHERN CALIFORNIA

This chapter will not include the geology of the Sierra Nevada as I covered that in my book on the Mother Lode. We will concern ourselves with the area of northwestern California and, to some degree, with the Modoc Plateau region.

Although geologists have worked sporadically in the area since the late 1800s, northwestern California is geologically one of the least known areas in the state. The eastern part of the area, where the greatest economic activity has been, was studied the most in the early days. The geology of the provinces of northwestern California differ greatly in their mineral deposits, geologic history, and topography.

The Klamath Mountains province is an area of rugged mountains with many peaks over 6,000 feet and some as high as nearly 9,000 feet with evidence of glaciation found in the higher elevations. The Klamath Mountains province is drained mainly by the Klamath and Smith Rivers. Most of the other drainage is by tributaries of the Klamath River and is generally from east to west. The principal rock units of these mountains range from early Paleozoic to middle-late Jurassic in age and are intruded by granitic rocks that range from hornblende diorite to true granite. The entire mountain mass is essentially an irregular and deeply dissected uplifted plateau. In many respects, the Klamath Mountains are similar to the Sierra Nevadas and are sometimes classified together as a single province in regards to certain geological aspects.

The northern Coast Ranges are mainly lower, and only along the main divide between the Coast Ranges and the Sacramento Valley drainage do any of its peaks reach as high as 6,000 feet and show any signs of glaciation. The

3

main rivers of the Coast Ranges are the Russian, Mad, Eel, and Van Duzen. The principal rocks range from late Jurassic to Cretaceous in age and there is little evidence that they have been intruded by granitic rocks.

The Sacramento Valley, an orderly pile of shale, graywacke and conglomerate, has been divided into Knoxville formation of late Jurassic age, the Shasta series of early Cretaceous age, and upper Cretaceous rocks. Sedimentary rocks of Tertiary age occur in both the northern Coast Ranges and the Klamath Mountains and cover an extensive area along the west side of the Sacramento Valley. Volcanic rocks of Quaternary age are abundant only at Clear Lake in the northern Coast Ranges.

The structure of northwestern California is highly complex and not well known. The boundary between the Coast Ranges and the western Klamath Mountains is a high-angle reverse fault that for most of its length is nearly parallel to the faults of the San Andreas system. The southern boundary of the Klamath Mountains province is a transverse fault that is aligned with major transverse faults in the Sacramento Valley and the Coast Ranges.

Gold ranks as the main mineral product of northwestern California with production estimated at over $150,000,000 since the Gold Rush. At today's price this would be the equivalent to $700,000,000–$800,000,000. Large quantities of gold have been produced from both placer and lode deposits mainly from the Klamath Mountains. Copper has also been found here and all but one of the most productive mines have been in the Klamath Mountains. Important amounts of quicksilver have been produced here from several deposits in the Coast Ranges and one in the Klamath Mountains. In 1894, gold production reached an early peak of over $3,000,000 a year that decreased to less than $1,000,000 a year during the 1920s. Both an increase in the price of gold from $20.67 to $35.00 and the Great Depression brought people back to rivers and streams in the 1930s with production rising to

4

$5,500,000 in 1941. The Second World War caused most of the mines to close and after the war it had gotten too expensive to open the mines.

The increase to the free market value spurred production again. Nearly all the gold deposits in northwestern California are in the Klamath Mountains and that province ranks second only to the Sierra Nevada in total gold production in California. Gold was the first metal sought and is said to have been discovered by Major Reading on the Trinity River, at what is now called Douglas City, in 1848. The gold comes from three main sources: placer deposits, lode deposits, and as a by-product of copper mining. During the first few years, almost all the gold came from working the placer deposits. Lode mining began in 1852 at the Washington Mine. Even with the discovery and working of the lode deposits for many years, most of the gold produced came from the placer deposits both in the gravels and the benches. During the period 1903 to 1932, approximately 1,602,000 ounces of gold were produced from placer deposits and 383,000 fine ounces were produced by the lode mines. The gold from this region averages about 850 fine.

The placer deposits are located along the Trinity and Klamath Rivers and their tributaries, other areas like Clear Creek, and the beaches along the coast. The placer deposits are a result of erosion of the gold bearing ores of the Klamath Mountains and their transportation and concentration by gravity and weather. Detrital gold occurs in most of the sedimentary formations of Tertiary and Quaternary ages in this area as well. The placer gold comes from lode deposits of the rocks of late Jurassic and older ages. The richest placer deposits of gold are those of Quaternary age, found in the gravels in the bench deposits and present streambeds along the streams. This is a result of repeated reconcentration of gold from sedimentary rocks of the Tertiary and Quaternary periods as they were eroded, but also added to each cycle was gold derived directly from the erosion of gold bearing lodes.

5

The placer deposits are found in the largest numbers in the areas of the most abundant lode deposits and in the streams that flow through those areas. Because the streams pick up the eroded gold and carry it until it is dropped and a deposit formed, the placer deposits are more widespread than the lode deposits. Even though most of the deposits are in the Klamath Mountains province, there are lode and placer gold deposits in the northern Coast Ranges, but until now they have not been as productive as the ones in the Klamaths. Sediments that reach the ocean have been winnowed to form deposits in the beach sands along the northern coast. Most of the gold that is found in the beach sands probably came from the erosion of sedimentary rocks of Tertiary and Quaternary ages that occur in the area. The gold in the beach sands is mostly very fine and large scale production has not been very productive.

Lode or ore deposits are rock masses from which metals are obtained commercially. Few ore deposits contain metals. Most are rock bodies containing one or more minerals in which the metallic element is combined with other elements. If the combination is such that the metal sought can be mined commercially, the rock is called ore or a lode deposit. The valuable minerals that contain the gold are called ore minerals. The ore minerals are separated from the useless minerals or, as they are called, the gangue minerals. All the rock that is separated from the valuable material is called, by some, waste rock. Most of the principal lode deposits are found in the acuate belt that parallels the gross structural grain in the central part of the Klamath Mountains. They are mainly in weakly metamorphosed sedimentary and volcanic rocks of Paleozoic age and most are associated with dike-like bodies of fine-grained intrusive igneous rocks known as "birds-eye" porphyry by the miners. In addition to the "birds-eye" porphyry, dikes of quartz porphyry are associated with the lode gold deposits found in the southwestern portion of this region. The mineral composition of the veins do not vary greatly. Quartz is the chief gangue mineral; mica and calcite are also present in small amounts. The gold occurs mainly as free gold but also in sulfide minerals. Pyrite, sphalerite, arsenopyrite, and galena and in some cases chalcopyrite are the sulfides. Lode gold deposits are found throughout the Klamath Mountains. The most productive district lode gold has been the French Gulch-Deadwood district of Shasta and Trinity Counties in the southern portion of the region. There has been a great deal of hydraulic mining in northwestern California and the La Grange mine west of Weaverville was one of the largest hydraulic mines in the state. There is still a lot of gold to be found in this region. Geologists think that some of the mines shut down before all the gold bearing ore was recovered and could be profitable if they are dug deeper.

The Modoc Plateau and Great Basin Region comprises about 16,000 square miles of northeastern California and has not produced a lot of gold, but there have been a few good mines worked there. There are not a large variety of rocks found here as it is made up mostly of Cenozoic basalt, andesite and local lake-laid sedimentary rocks. Minor amounts of copper and quicksilver are found here as well. The gold veins are found in volcanic rocks of Tertiary age. The veins range from one to as much as twenty-five feet in thickness and none has gone too deep.

The placer deposits are replenished every rainy season and there are still new lode deposits to be found and even old mines to reopen in Northern California. So you can see that the prospects are good for you to find some of that gold and well worth your while to get out and look for it.

Hydraulic mining in the 1860's, Michigan Bar District. This is a view of hydraulic mining and ground sluicing in Sacramento County over 100 years ago. The locomotive headlights at right made nighttime floodlights. (Courtesy of California State Library)

2. Geology of Placer Deposits

In order to have the best chance at finding that golden dream you are seeking, you need to have some knowledge of placer deposits. A lot of our information comes from the early miners and prospectors who climbed, dug into, and checked out most every mountain, canyon, stream, river, and creek in this great state. This is still the best method, as geologists admit that even today they don't know everything there is to know about the remaining rich gravel deposits. A Mineral Information Service Bulletin put out by The State of California Division of Mines and Geology stated, "The geologic history and structure of the buried channels are so complex that the best of engineers have been baffled by them. Fragmentary benches and segments of rich gravel deposits which still rest in positions completely hidden from the surface, or even from the underground passages which enter into the lower main channels, afford alluring possibilities to the geologist as well as the prospector." So they are telling us that there is still a lot of gold out there and you've as good a chance at finding it as any geologist.

The number one thing to keep in mind is that most all areas have been prospected at one time or the other. Don't waste a lot of time in areas that have not proven to be productive in the past. Search the areas that are known to be gold bearing and take advantage of the knowledge gained by those who went before you.

There are several types of placer deposits which are classified here to indicate how they were first formed. The basic placers are:

(1) Residual placers or "Seam Diggings."

(2) Elovial or hillside placers, representing transitional creep from residual deposits to stream gravels.

(3) Bajada placers, a name given to a peculiar type of desert or dry placers.

(4) Stream placers, which have been sorted and resorted, and are simple and well merged.

(5) Glacial stream placers which are for the most part profitless.

(6) Eolian placers, or local concentrations caused by the removal of lighter materials by the wind.

(7) Marine or beach placers.

Of the seven types, the stream placer is the most important. They have been the source of most of the placer gold mined in California. Stream placers consist of sands and gravels sorted by the action of running water. If they have undergone several periods of erosion, and have been re-sorted, the greater the concentration of the heavier minerals. Deposits by streams include those of both present and ancient times, whether they form well defined channels or are left merely as benches. All bench placers, when first laid down, were stream placers similar to those of the present stream deposits. If not reworked by later erosion, they are left as terraces or benches on the sides of the valley cut by the present stream. These deposits are called bench gravels. In order to understand stream placers, streams themselves must be studied in regard to their habit, history, and character.

Residual placers are formed when the gold is released from its source and the encasing material broken down. This is most effectively done by long continued surface weathering. Disintegration is accomplished by persistent and powerful geologic conditions which effect the mechanical breaking down of the rock and the chemical decay of the minerals. The surface of a gold bearing ore body is enriched during this process of rock disintegration, because some of the softer and more soluble parts of the rock are carried away by erosion.

After gold is released from its bedrock encasement by rock decay and weathering, it begins to creep down the hillside and may be washed down rivulets and gullies and into the streambeds. On its way down the hillside the gold is sometimes concentrated in sufficient value to warrant mining. These deposits are classified as Elovial Deposits.

It is a common fallacy of some prospectors to attribute the forming of some placer deposits to the action of glaciers. Since it is the habit of glaciers to scrape off loose soil and debris but not to sort it, ice is ineffective in the concentration of metals. The streams issuing from the melting ice may sometimes be effective enough in sorting to create a deposit.

Bajada is a spanish word for slope and is used to identify a confluent alluvial fan along the base of a mountain range. The total production of gold from bajada placers is small compared to other placer workings due to the less efficient dry washing methods used in the past. The forming of a bajada placer is basically similar to a stream placer except as it is conditioned by the climate and topography of the arid region in which it occurs. The bulk of the gold that has been released from its matrix as it travels from the lode outcrop to the bajada slope is deposited on the slope close to the mountain range. The gold is dropped along the lag line which is the contact of the basin fill with the bedrock. Although the heaviest concentration of gold will be on bedrock, bulk concentration does not occur as in a stream deposit. Since a certain percentage of gold is still locked in its matrix there is a strong tendency for less gold to reach bedrock and for more to remain distributed throughout the deposit than in the case of stream gravels.

There have been several beach placers found and worked along the Pacific Coast. Beach placers are a result of the shore currents and wave action on the materials broken down from the sea cliffs or washed into the sea by streams. There are two types of beach placers–present beaches and ancient beaches. Most of the gold bearing beaches are found in northern California. Not a great deal of production has come from these deposits. Most of the gold will come from the rocks that are being eroded by the waves.

Most of the Eolian placers of the desert are as a result of the bajada being enriched on the surface by wind action on the lighter materials.

There are several things that occur to preserve a placer deposit. Since streams are constantly changing their position, fragments of their deposits are left isolated; for example, the beaches and terraces that are left at different intervals when a stream is cutting a deeper channel. These deposits that are left will eventually be eroded away unless something protects them. Burial is the most effective way a placer may be preserved. Mostly when the name "buried channel" is given to a placer it is one where a stream has been covered by lava, mud flows, ash falls etc. There are other ways by which they may be buried such as:

(1) By covering with landslide material.

(2) By covering with gravel.

(3) By covering with lake deposits.

(4) By covering with gravel when the stream is choked.

(5) By covering with gravel when the stream course is lowered below the general base level of erosion.

(6) By the covering of older stream courses with alluvial fan material, as conditions favorable to stream existence fail.

(7) By covering with glacial till.

(8) By covering of beach placers with marine sediments as the coast is submerged and elevated.

The gravel content of a placer may become firmly cemented when it is infiltrated by mineral matter, such as lime, iron carbonate, or silica. The older the placer, the more likely this is to occur. These cemented gravels

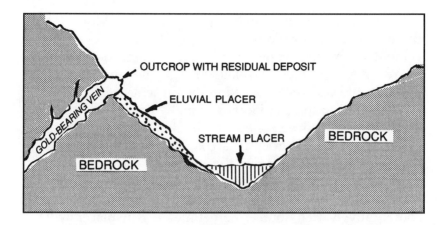

Most gold comes from intrusive veins, which break up to form eluvial deposits. These deposits move downhill until captured by moving water, which continues the separation of gold from its original rock matrix.

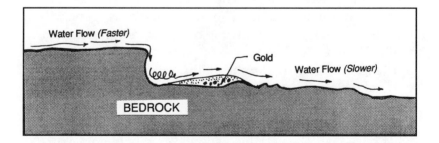

Any feature of a stream bed that suddenly slows the flow of water may cause the water to drop heavy gold particles. Look around the base of a fall for a deposit of heavy minerals and gold.

sometimes are very hard to break down. This is why some of the tailings in the old mines are profitable to work. The cemented gravels sometimes were never completely broken down as they traveled through the sluice boxes, and the gold was re-deposited in the present streambed.

The gold found in placers originally came from veins and other mineralized zones in bedrock when the gold was released from its rock matrix by weathering and disintegration. Many times the source of the gold in a placer would not be a deposit that could be mined at a profit, but the richer deposits usually indicate a comparatively rich source. Sometimes a rich placer will develop when several low grade veins feed it over a very long time. The richest placers are created when there is reconcentration from older gold bearing gravels. For the most part, the original source of the gold is not far from the place where it was first deposited after being carried by running water.

The mineral grains that are very heavy and resistant to mechanical and chemical destruction will be found with the gold in placer deposits. These are what prospectors and miners call black sand. The black sand is generally principally magnetite, but some of the other minerals you will find in your sluice box are garnet, zircon, hematite, pyrite (fool's gold), chromite, platinum, cinnabar, tungsten minerals, titanium minerals, as well as diamonds.

You'll find a lot of other things such as quicksilver, metallic copper, amalgam, nails, buckshot, B.B.s, bullets and what have you. The very high specific gravity of gold, six or seven times that of quartz, and increasing to nine times under water, is what causes the gold to work its way to the bedrock or false bedrock, or any point that it can go no further. Once it is trapped on bedrock, the stream has great difficulty picking it up again. The specific gravity of gold is 19, that is, it weighs 19 times as much as a equal amount of water to its mass.

14

AVERAGE SPECIFIC GRAVITY OF SOME MINERALS

Mica	2.3
Feldspar	2.5
Quartz	2.7
Hornblende	3.2
Garnet	3.5
Corundum	4.0
Magnetite	5.2
Silver	7.5
Gold	19.2

Due to its insolubility, the finest particles of gold are preserved. A piece of gold worth less than a quarter can easily be recognized in a pan. Since gold is so malleable it will be hammered into different shapes by stones as they tumble along in the stream. It will not be welded together to form larger nuggets as some people believe. Particles of gold may be broken down, however, from another piece. Geologists have shown that the largest masses of gold come from lodes and not placers. The more rounded and flattened nuggets that you find have probably been in the stream for a longer amount of time and have taken more knocking around than the ones that show the original crystalline form. The crystalline nuggets are known as course gold and probably have not traveled as far from the source in the free state.

The gold found in the more ancient placers have a higher degree of fineness than those whose source is nearby. This may be due to the removal of alloyed silver by the dissolving action of the water. The accumulation of gold in an important placer deposit is not just pure coincidence, but is the result of some fortunate circumstances. In areas where nature has provided extensive mineralization, rapid rock decay, and well-developed stream patterns, there is the opportunity for large amounts of gold placers to be formed.

Basically what happens is fairly simple. In areas where the gold has been deposited, the power of the stream has become insufficient to carry off the particles of gold that have settled.

How rich the deposit is will depend on how complete the loss of transporting power is, as well as the ability of the bedrock to hold the deposited gold, plus the general relationship of the gold sources to the stream.

When a stream is eroding, the materials in reach of its activity are constantly moved downstream. During this movement a constant sorting is taking place, which causes a concentration of the heavier particles.

Disposition then takes place in the stream when the velocity is decreased, either by changes in volume or grade. When this happens the gold is laid down with the other sediments. Sometimes the placer gold may be trapped in irregularities in the bedrock, without considerable detritus material being trapped with it; but extensive placers, as a rule, are not formed by irregularities in the bedrock alone.

When the bed of the stream is the actual rock floor of the valley, this is true bedrock. When the gravels become covered with volcanic or other materials, the stream will flow over this new floor making deposits on what is known as false bedrock.

So you can see that an area may contain two or more layers of gold bearing gravels. An easy way to see how a stream lays down these various layers is to study areas where road cuts have exposed ancient stream deposits and also in the canyons where the benches can be seen.

A smooth hard bedrock is a very poor one to develop a good placer deposit. The bedrock formations that are highly decomposed and possess cracks and crevices are good, and those of a clay-like or schistose nature are rated excellent in their ability to trap the gold.

To give you an idea of the carrying power of a stream, here are some figures from a report by the California Division of Mines and Geology on the size of material carried by a stream flowing at different velocities:

3 in. per sec. — 0.170mph will just begin to work on fine clay.

6 in. per sec. — 0.340mph will lift fine sand.

8 in. per sec. — 0.4545mph will lift sand as coarse as linseed.

10 in. per sec. — 0.5mph will lift gravel the size of peas.

12 in. per sec. — 0.6819mph will sweep along gravel the size of beans.

24 in. per sec. — 1.3638mph will roll along rounded pebbles 1 inch in diameter.

3 ft. per sec. — 2.045mph will sweep along
slippery angular stones the size of hens eggs.

As far as grade is concerned, a grade ranging from 30 to approximately 100 feet per mile will favor the disposition of gold. Anywhere that the grade is greater than that, such as in mountain streams, or in narrow canyons, will not be a good source of placer deposits.

When a stream leaves its mountain canyons and enters a more level country or a still body of water, the material carried by the stream is deposited in the form of a fan or a delta. At the apex of this fan or delta the fine gold will be deposited, and may never reach bed rock. The stirring action that occurs in the rugged mountains during times of floods, which permits gold to reach bedrock, does not take place in the delta.

To sum things up, remember that the gold is heavy, heavier than most of the other material in the streambed and it will drop anywhere the flow or grade changes causing the stream to slow down or lose its carrying power. These are the places you want to search. Each rainy season

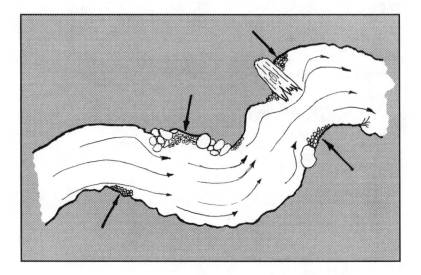

Obstructions in a stream's path that slow the flow of water are likely areas for gold to be deposited. Look on the inside of curves in a stream as well as around large obstructions like rocks or fallen tree trunks.

will bring new gold down from the hillsides into the streambed. Another thing to keep in mind is the fact that the early miners were working deposits that had thousands of years to develop. Try to find material that has not been worked before or try to reach the hard-to-get to areas where the chances are that the gravels have not been worked as much. The most important thing to keep in mind is that **"Gold is there to be found!"**

3. WHERE TO FIND GOLD
BUTTE COUNTY

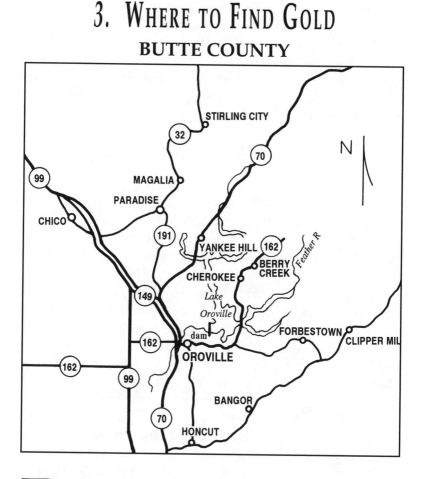

utte County is one of the original counties in the state. The first county seat was at the mining camp of Hamilton but when the diggings there played out, the county seat was moved to Bidwell's Bar and then to Oroville in 1856. Gold was found here early in the Gold Rush. John Bidwell was working the placer deposits on the Feather River as early as July of 1848, at what later became known as Bidwell's Bar. As the deposits played out at Bidwell's Bar, the miners moved on down the river to the new diggings at Ophir City, whose name became Oroville later on. Some of this area is covered in my book, *Where To Find Gold In The Mother Lode*. Butte County has a rich mining history and is still producing gold for prospectors. All parts of the Feather River and most all of the creeks here have produced gold at some time. Try your luck in any of the gold district locations listed here and you will be rewarded to some degree.

BANGOR

This is also called the Wyandette district by some miners. A large placer gold mining area, it was first discovered in the early Gold Rush period. The district is in southeastern Butte County around the old mining camp sites of Bangor and Wyandette. Wyandette was named for Wyandette Indians who mined there. The camps reached their peaks in the mid-1850s. Today, some of the old mining ditches are used to irrigate the farm lands. A large amount of hydraulic and drift mining was done here clear up into the 1890s. The Chinese miners were active here beginning in the 1870s. There are gold bearing Tertiary channel gravels here covering an area about three by eight miles that were once a part of the ancient Yuba River. The gold is found in the recent gravels as well. Some large nuggets have been found in this district in the past. One was said to weigh 14 pounds, so bring your metal detector with you when you work this district. Take the Oroville-Bangor road southeast out of Oroville to reach this area.

BIDWELL'S BAR

Bidwell's Bar is located on the middle fork of the Feather River about 39 miles above the town of Marysville. Most of this district is now under Oroville Lake. Mostly a placer mining district it also includes the Stringtown, Hurleton, Enterprise areas. Stringtown, about four miles east of Bidwell's Bar, was so-called for the fact that the buildings were strung out in a wandering narrow line in the canyon. When it became a ghost town in 1856, a paper wrote, "the string of Stringtown has been pulled out." When news of Bidwell's rich find here got out, a rush to the area began and camps sprang up all over the area at places such as Adamstown, Long's Bar, Potter's Bar, and Thompson Flat. All the old camps have disappeared. The gold is found in the recent gravels as well as the ancient gravels dating from the Pleistocene age. A few small gold-quartz veins have been found here but most of the production has come from the placer deposits. You can reach this area by taking Highway 162 east out of Oroville.

CHEROKEE

This district is also known as the Spring Valley district. Named for a group of Cherokee Indians who mined here early in the 1850s, the town reached its peak in the 1870s. Most all of the production of $15,000,000 has come from one source, the Spring Valley Gold Mine. It was at one time the largest hydraulic mine in California. The gold is found in Tertiary gravels on the north side of Table Mountain. These are some of the famous rich blue quartz gravels sought by prospectors for their rich gold content. You want to be on the lookout for diamonds when working here. It is estimated that somewhere between 300 to 500 diamonds have come from these diggings. Most are of industrial quality, but heck, as far as I'm concerned a diamond is a diamond. Platinum has also been found here. Take Highway 70 north from Oroville, the Cherokee area is on your right just before you get to the lake.

CLIPPER MILLS

This district is located in both Butte and Yuba Counties. It is a placer and lode gold area. The placer gold is found mainly in the Tertiary gravels found here. A lot of the gold has been recovered by hydraulic mining but there has been some drift mining done as well. This is a good area for pocket miners as the gold-quartz veins, though not very big, have been rich in spots. To reach Clipper Mills, go north on Highway 70 out of Marysville to Ramirez Road and go east and north until you reach La Porte Road. Take La Porte Road to Clipper Mills.

FORBESTOWN

Forbestown was one of the richest placer mining areas of the early Gold Rush. It is located on the south fork of the Feather River. The town was established in 1850 when Ben Forbes opened a store here. It was a center of mining activity for almost 40 years. Old Forbestown was about a mile north of the present site. During the rush it was a center of cultural activity for the miners with a general assembly hall and a private academy, as well as the location of the Sunday services. The Feather Falls area is also included in this district. There are a few gold-quartz veins found here, as well as the placer deposits. Dredgers have done well here as new gold is washed in every rainy season. Take Highway 162 east out of Oroville to the Forbestown Road. Take this road to Forbestown.

HONCUT

Honcut is mainly a bucket and dragline dredging district. The placers were first worked by hand in the early days but after that the production was almost all from dredging along Honcut and Wilson Creeks. The creeks are tributaries to the Yuba River. The district is located in southwest Butte County. Go north on Highway 70 to Lower Honcut Road. Go east on this road to reach this area. It is before you get to Ramirez Road.

INSKIP

Inskip is mainly a lode mining district with a small amount of placer gold being found here. It is located in northwestern Butte County. Now the camp is best known for its hotel that was built in 1869, and is listed in the National Register of Historical Places. The gold-quartz veins occur in slate, greenstone, and amphibolite. The veins are small but productive. Take Skyway Road east off of Highway 99, south of Chico. This will take you past Paradise and Sterling City. Inskip is about seven miles past Sterling City.

KIMSHEW

This district is in both Butte and Plumas Counties. It also includes the Golden Summit area. Kimshew is both a lode and placer mining district. The gold is found in both the ancient Tertiary and recent gravels. Most of the production of the placers has come from hydraulic mining. There have been a few gold-quartz veins worked here as well. The Concow Road off of Highway 70, north of Lake Oroville, will take you into this area.

MAGALIA

This district is most famous for the 54-pound nugget found here. It is known as the Magalia or Dogtown Nugget and was discovered in 1859. The camp was first known as Dogtown because of the large number of dogs kept here by a French woman. The nugget was found two miles east of the town and the site is marked by a historical landmark monument. The district is in north central Butte County. This is both a placer and lode mining district and includes the gold bearing gravels at Forks of Butte Mineral Side, Nimshew and De Sabla. The placer deposits were discovered early in the Gold Rush and the town was established in 1850. It still survives today.

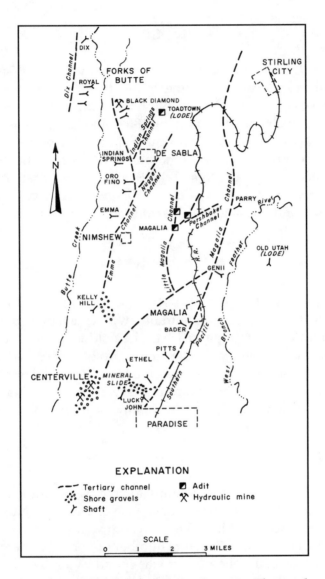

Map of Magalia District, Butte County. The northern part of Butte Creek district is also shown. The channels are not all the same geological age.
(Reprinted by permission, from California Division of Mines and Geology, *Gold Districts of California*, 88)

Mining has gone on here continuously since the first piece of gold was panned out here. This is one of the most productive placer mining districts in the state which is saying something. The gold bearing area reaches from the west branch of the Feather River to Butte Creek and from the town of Paradise on the south to the town of Stirling City on the north. There are several gold bearing Tertiary gravel channels found here. The biggest channel is the Mammoth or Magalia channel which is on the east side of the district. The other productive channels are the Little Magalia, Nugger, Emma, Dix, and Pershbaker. Most of the gold found here is very coarse and makes good specimens pieces. There have been quite a few other large nuggets found here and it is a good location for nugget shooting. Some gold-quartz veins have been worked here as well. Estimates of the gold production go as high as $40,000,000 for the district. This district has had a lot of real estate development and, sadly, many good prospects have been built over by developers. Take Skyway north out of Paradise. This road goes right through the area.

MORRIS RAVINE

This is both a lode and placer mining district. It is located on the south side of Oroville Table Mountain, three miles north of Oroville. All the ravines in this area were first worked in the Gold Rush by placer mining. This also includes the Monte de Oro area. As the first rich placer gravels began to play out, the miners started searching for the lode deposits and a few narrow gold-quartz veins were discovered and developed. The veins are not high grade but do contain some rich pockets. Work has continued on and off since the Gold Rush in Morris Ravine. The ancient gravels contain a great deal of fine course gold in places. A few diamonds have also been found here so keep your eyes open for them. This area is on the north side of the Feather River in the region between the fish hatchery and the Oroville Dam.

Cherokee Mining Company Dredge, Oroville District. This 1904 photo shows one of the earliest bucket-like dredges in California, operating here in Butte County. (Reprinted, by permission, from California Division of Mines and Geology, Gold Districts of California, 104)

OROVILLE

The first miners here were 49'ers and the camp was first known as Ophir City. The name was changed to Oroville in 1856. There were several other camps here such as Thompson Flat, and a hill here still bears that name. Another camp was Centerville or Middletown, which was located about where the present Southern Pacific station, is now in Oroville. Hydraulic mining began here as early as the 1850s and continued for several years. You can still see evidence of the hydraulicking in the channels, ditches, scarred hills, and old flumes remaining here. It is said that gold dredging originated here and bucket line dredging has been the biggest producer of gold here. The dredging field is nearly two miles wide and nine miles long. At one time, there were 35 dredges working here and dredging alone has produced over 1,964,000 ounces of gold from this area. One dredging company even offered to move the whole town of Oroville and rebuild it at the company's expense so that it could dredge beneath the town and remove the golden earth that the town has been built over. Talk about your streets paved with gold, well here it is folks. At one time, Oroville had one of the largest Chinatowns in California with an estimated population of 10,000 Chinese living there. The gold is found in the river gravels and terrace deposits on the flood plain. Oroville is located in southwest Butte County on Highway 70.

YANKEE HILL

The stream and surface gravels were first worked in the early part of the Gold Rush and paid fairly well. First known as Spanishtown, the deposits were discovered by Spanish speaking miners from Chile and Mexico. It was also called Rich Gulch and then, finally, Yankee Hill. It had a reputation as a wild and wooly camp in its day. It includes the Concow and Big Bend areas as well. The lode

27

mining began in the 1850s and continued off and on until 1942 when the war closed down much of the mines everywhere. At least 100,000 ounces of gold has been taken out of this area mostly from the lode deposits. The Chinese miners reworked the gravels here after the Gold Rush years sometimes getting more gold than the original miners. The lode deposits are mostly gold-quartz veins and are found in metamorphic rocks. Old Yankee Hill is about a mile east of Highway 70 and a mile south of new Yankee Hill.

TREASURE TALE

There is said to be a lost mine near Oroville. According to the story told, an Indian would bring a bag full of nuggets into town every few months . He said he had a mine full of the nuggets but just took what he needed to live on. He said he could live to be a hundred and never run out of nuggets. He said he hid his mine each time he left it and no one could find it. He was right, because even when some of miners tried to follow him he would lose them every time. On his last trip into Oroville he became sick and died. Some stories say he drank himself to death. When he left town he always went north. Someday the elements will expose his hidden mine and some lucky treasure hunter will find it. Keep your eyes open out there.

ROCK AND GEM SITES

Road cuts on Highway 70 have exposed a great deal of serpentine suitable for polishing and carving. There is some pure dark green but most is varicolored. Don't be afraid of the multicolor pieces because they can be quite beautiful when polished. Like most serpentine, some of the material can be flaky but you can find solid pieces here. The collecting location is along side Highway 70, north out of Oroville about 18 miles from its split with Highway 149.

HISTORICAL SITES

The Dogtown Nugget Discovery site monument is located about 1/3 mile north of Pentz-Magalia Road on Skyway. This also known as the Magalia Nugget. If one was found there, there must be more. Any good prospector would want to go there and say, "If only."

DEL NORTE COUNTY

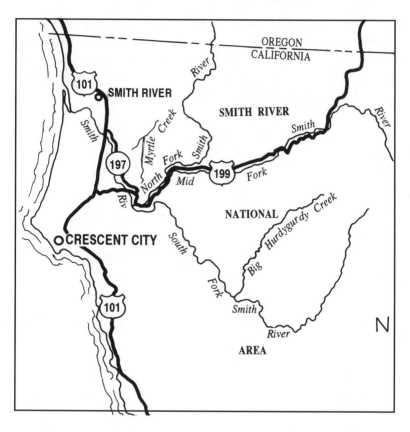

This county was created from a portion of Klamath County in 1857. Del Norte is Spanish for "of the north" and it sure is. It is located in the far northwestern part of California. It is interesting that Klamath County is the only California county to be dissolved. The first miners had come to the Trinity River from the Sacramento Valley and spread to this area looking for new gold deposits and a more direct access to the sea. As the number of miners increased, the mining camp of Klamath city was established in 1851, near the mouth of the Klamath River. It was hoped that it would be a port of entry to the back country but the shifting sandbars made navigation uncertain and the city was a ghost by late 1852. This area was always closely associated with southwestern Oregon and before the boundary line between the states was established, the miners all considered themselves Californians. When told of the boundary line decision, the miners were upset because it was said that they had always voted in California and Oregon and refused to pay taxes to either.

There are quite a few streams in the county that have produced gold in various amounts over the years, such as Bluff Creek, Notice Creek, Patrick Creek, Hardscrabble Creek, and others. Try your luck in any of the creeks connected to the Smith River and you should find some gold. There are three principal gold districts in Del Norte County.

CRESCENT CITY

Crescent City was established as a port for ships bringing supplies to the miners in 1853. The bay was first seen by searchers for the "Lost Cabin Mine" in 1851. Rich diggings were found around Crescent City in 1854, and in 1855, the miners on Myrtle Creek, 12 miles northwest of the city, were making $15 a day. New diggings were found on the south fork of the Smith River and miners were making $20 a day there. In 1854, discoveries were made six miles from Crescent City in a creek that enters the Smith River at White and Miller Ferry, which was known later as Peacock's Ferry. Mining claims were even staked on the beach in front of the city. Gold was found in the Bald Hills east of the city and a camp named Villardville was set up. Other camps around Crescent Bay that are now gone were Big Flat, Altaville, Low Divide, Redwood Diggings, Hurdygurdy Creek, Growler Gulch, and others whose names have been forgotten. Gold and minor amounts of platinum have been recovered from the beaches south of Crescent City. Most of the gold recovered from the beach deposits has come from small scale operations. They have tried to mine the sands on a large scale but they have proven unsuccessful. Most of the gold in the beach sands has probably been deposited there by the Klamath and Smith Rivers. Crescent City is on Highway 101.

MONUMENTAL

The Monumental district is a small lode gold district. Most of the production has come from one source, the Monumental Consolidated mine. The gold-quartz veins occur in greenstone and slate and have not run to great depths. There has been some copper mined here with gold as a by-product. The Monumental district is 45 miles northeast of Crescent City.

SMITH RIVER

This is the most productive district in Del Norte County. The majority of the gold produced has come from working the placer deposits of the Smith River and its tributaries. Some of the best diggings were at French Hill, Craig's Creek, Myrtle Creek, Monkey Creek, and Hurdygurdy Creek. The gold is found in the present stream gravels, as well as in bench deposits along side the streams. Most of the bench or terrace gravels were worked by hydraulicking. The largest production came in the early years, as in most districts, but there has been work done here with modest results right up to today. This is a good area for the modern prospector to check out. It is estimated that the area has produced over 40,000 ounces of gold. The main area is about eight miles north of Crescent City. Take Highway 101 north out of Crescent City to Highway 199, to the junction with 197. Begin here and take the South Fork Road a little farther east to reach the south fork diggings.

TREASURE TALES

The oldest and most told treasure tale of Del Norte County is the story of the Lost Cabin Treasure. According to the story, one of the very first miners in the Gold Rush came into this area long before anyone else and struck it rich. He built a cabin in the wilderness so that he could stay long enough to amass a fortune and return to his family in the east. He worked every day for months and his store of gold grew to the point that he was almost ready to pack up and head home. It was then that Lady Luck failed him. A band of marauding Indians discovered his cabin. They attacked the lone miner and left him for dead after burning down his cabin and taking his supplies. He had hidden his gold and they didn't find it. He was able to recover from the attack but his mind was confused. All he wanted to do was get away from the threat of the Indians. Somehow he was able to reach civilization but he had left his gold behind. He told friends they were welcome to it if they wanted to face death to get it and even drew a crude map showing that the cabin site was obviously in upper north-western California in the Coast Ranges in the area of what is now Del Norte County.

HISTORICAL SITE

Camp Lincoln was a U.S. military post set up to keep peace between the Indians and the miners and settlers in 1862. I always enjoy visiting historical locations while on a prospecting trip. Somehow, being at the places where the early prospectors and miners made history makes you feel like you're still a part of the past. Those men and women were doing just what you're doing; looking for gold and making history at the same time.

HUMBOLDT COUNTY

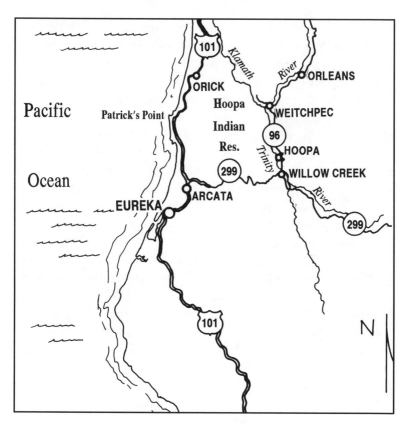

There has been some good gold found here. This is mainly a placer mining area with the gold being found in the present stream gravels and the older bench deposits. The county was established in 1853 and Uniontown (now Arcata) was made the county seat. There was quite a bit of trouble here between the miners and the Indians. The coast Indians got along with the miners but the mountain Indians resented the settlers taking land they considered theirs. There was killing on both sides and the government had to send in the army and establish Fort Humboldt to keep the peace in 1853.

HOOPA

This district is mainly in the Hoopa Valley Indian Reservation and you need to get permission to prospect here. There was some placer mining done here on the Trinity River during the Gold Rush. Most of the production has come as a by-product from copper mining at the Copper Bluff copper mine since then. The placer deposits are found in the present stream gravels and the terrace along the river. The ore deposits consist of mineralized schist and quartz veins containing gold. Try your luck in the creeks and streams near the reservation, as most contain gold to some degree. Take Highway 96 north off of Highway 299 at Willow Creek to reach this area.

ORICK

This district is also known as Gold Bluff Beach. Mineable gold placer deposits in beach sands are somewhat rare but the deposits here have produced over $1,000,000. The gold bearing black sands stretch along the ocean beach for a distance of almost 10 miles. The beaches were first mined in 1852, and active mining continued into the 1880s. The deposits have been mined on and off since then. Gold and small amounts of platinum occur in thin but sometimes large layers of black sands on the beach. The bench and terrace gravels in the bluffs east of the beach also contain gold. The gold in black sand is deposited by wave action and shore currents that work on the materials broken down from the sea cliffs and gold that is carried into the ocean by the streams. The Klamath River has probably brought a lot of the gold that is found here from where it empties into the ocean a few miles north of Gold Beach. The gold is very fine grained and the fineness runs as high as 950. Miners have used every gold recovering devise you can think of to work the sands including a sluice designed just for surf washing. Another interesting fact is that you can find some placer platinum here, so keep your eyes open. Orick is on Highway 101 about 50 miles north of Arcata.

ORLEANS BAR

This district is known as just Orleans now but originally was named Orleans Bar. It was once an important mining center, and was the county seat for the now disestablished Klamath County from 1855 to 1875 and is now a quiet village. The district is on the Klamath in the northeast corner of Humboldt County. This is a placer mining area and the gold bearing deposits are in the present stream gravels as well as in the older bench gravels. The paying bench gravels are found anywhere from 50 to 80 feet above the river bed. The bench deposits have been mined by hydraulicking in the past. You can also find some platinum here. Orleans is located on Highway 96 north of the Hoopa Valley Indian Reservation.

WEITCHPEC

This district is located at the junction of the Klamath River and the Trinity River. It is now included in both the Trinity River district and the Klamath River district and is no longer listed separately. It is a placer mining district and has been very productive in the past. The gold is found in the present stream gravels as well as in the older gravels in the benches. Weekend miners do quite well in this area. Weitchpec is on Highway 96, before you get to Orleans, at the junction of the two rivers.

WILLOW CREEK

This district is another district that has been lumped together with others and named the Trinity River District. That makes the Trinity River district quite spread out, so I continue to list them separately where I feel they were important enough to merit it. This was never a huge producing district but it has been steady. You can still get a little gold here and sometimes do quite well. Willow Creek is located at the junction of Highway 96 and Highway 299.

ROCK AND GEM SITES

As long as you're out, you might enjoy a little rockhounding. You can find green serpentine as well as collectable agate about five and a half miles west of Willow Creek off of Highway 299. The collecting area is on both sides of the creek here.

You can also collect agate at Patrick's Point State Park. Ask at the museum for directions to Agate Beach.

TREASURE TALE

The Lost Bell Treasure tale is told in Humboldt County. According to the story, a ship carrying a large shipment of gold to the San Francisco Mint ran aground in Shelter Cove. The ship was raided by renegades and the gold was stolen. Some of the raiders took the gold and hid it under a tree on a flat. When they returned for more loot they were caught by troops sent to look for the ship. A fight broke out and all the raiders were killed except for some women with them. They had used the ships bell to mark the tree under which the gold was buried. The women never told their captors about the bell until years later when one of them, now an old lady, confessed. Deer hunters are said to have found the bell in the tree and took it home not knowing its significance. Nobody has ever found the buried treasure.

HISTORICAL SITE

Fort Humboldt was established in 1853 to keep peace among the miners, Indians, and settlers. It was so dreary that Ulysses S. Grant spent only four and a half months here and resigned from the Army to return to his home in the east. The fort was abandoned sometime between 1867 and 1870. It is located on Highway 101 south of Eureka.

Divers moving boulders in order to dredge crevices that lie below. (Courtesy Keene Engineering)

LASSEN COUNTY

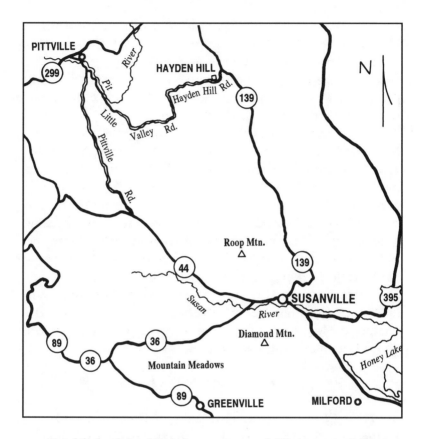

Established in 1854 from parts of Plumas and Shasta Counties, Lassen County was named for pioneer Peter Lassen. Lassen and a partner were killed on the morning of April 28, 1859, by Indians while on a prospecting trip in the Honey Lake area. Another man got away and was able to tell the story of Lassen's death. Susanville has always been the county seat. Up until recently, Lassen Gold Mining Inc. was one of the largest employers in the county.

Most of the gold production for the county has come from the Hayden Hill district but there is gold in other areas. The deposits are in both the Sierra Nevada and the Modoc Plateau province.

DIAMOND MOUNTAIN

The Diamond Mountain block is in the farthest north end of the Sierra Nevadas in southern Lassen County. This is both a placer mining area and lode mining area. The placers were not discovered until the late 1850s but still produced several hundred thousand dollars in gold. After the original miners worked the placers, the Chinese miners followed them and did a small amount of work here. Estimated production for the district is over $1,000,000. The first lode deposits were worked in the 1860s and production continued into the early 1900s. As with a lot of areas, the Depression of the 1930s brought people back into the region and production increased for awhile. The gold-quartz veins are as thick as 15 feet in some places and occur mainly in quartz diorite. There have been some high-grade pockets found here as well. Some of the veins also contain opal. The prospector-rockhound could be in heaven by finding a rich pocket of gold and opal here. The Diamond Mountains are on the west side of Highway 395, about five or six miles south of Susanville.

HAYDEN HILL

This the most important gold district in the Modoc Plateau Province. Lode gold was discovered here in the late 1860s and the mining camp of Providence City was established when gold seekers rushed to the new diggings. The name of the camp was changed to Hayden Hill in 1878. Fire destroyed most of the town in 1910. Mining continued off and on into the 1930s and prospectors still wander the area looking for that new strike. The district is in northwestern Lassen County. More than $3,000,000 in gold has been taken out of this area. Some of the veins are as thick as 25 feet and also contain silver. Take the Hayden Hill Road west four miles off of Highway 139 about sixty-five miles north of Susanville.

40

HONEY LAKE

A little mining and prospecting was done here as early as the Gold Rush. Best known for the fact Peter Lassen was killed here while prospecting and not for its gold, there have been small amounts of gold mined here. It was after the turn of the century that any real mining took place. The Honey Lake mine was discovered in 1900 and worked off and on into the 1930s. Part of this district is also in Plumas County. The gold quartz are mostly narrow and found in granite rock. There is no record of the gold production for the district. The Honey Lake mine is in the mountains west of Highway 395, a few miles south of Milford.

MOUNTAIN MEADOWS

Some gold has been recovered from the Tertiary gravels found here. It was a poor man's diggings, worked mainly in the early days. There is no record of the production for this district. The Tertiary gravels are found in the southeast portion of the valley and extend down to the Taylorville and Genesee District. The Mountain Meadows district is located eight miles northeast of Greenville off of Highway 89.

ROCK AND GEM SITES

You can find some beautiful banded rhyolite around the site of the old camp of Hayden Hill. The rhyolite is found all over and in all sizes. You can pick and choose the best pieces for polishing.

TREASURE TALES

Tiburcio Vasquez was a bandit who roamed all over California committing robbery and mayhem. According to one story, he and his men raided a stage-stop named

Kingston in Lassen County and held several men hostage while robbing several stores there. A fight broke out with the town people while they were trying to escape with the money from the robberies and the bandit carrying the loot was wounded. By the time he was able to get to where the bandits had hid their horses, everyone was gone. They must have thought he was dead because they took his horse with them. He hid in the rocks to avoid the angry mob chasing him but he probably died from his wounds, as a skeleton was found several years later in the rocks. He must have buried the loot because it wasn't with the skeleton. The loot has never been found. There is an area in Southern California known as Vasquez Rocks that was supposed to be one of Tiburcio's hideouts. The bandit leader was caught and hanged in Los Angeles later, but had very little money with him when captured. He claimed he would lead them to his hidden loot if they would set him free but they hanged him anyway.

There are said to be $20 gold pieces to be found along the Pit River a few miles from the Lassen-Shasta County line. They came from a wagon train that was ambushed there. The Indians had no use for the coins and took turns seeing who could throw them the longest distance across the river. People are said to find one of the coins every once in a while.

HISTORICAL SITES

You can visit the site of Peter Lassen's grave by going about three miles south out of Susanville on Richmond and Wingfield Roads.

When in Susanville visit Roop's Fort. It was here that Isaac Roop and about 20 other settlers tried to establish their own territory but failed. It is also the location of the so called "Sagebrush War" between citizens of this region and Plumas County officials.

PLUMAS COUNTY

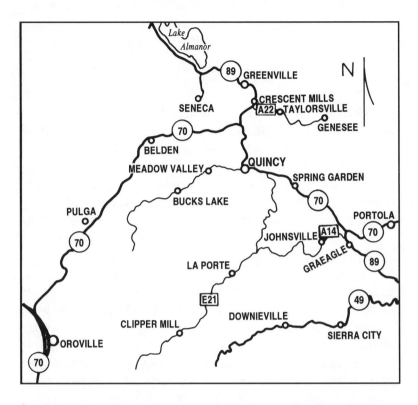

This is one of the most productive counties for gold in California. Estimated production for Plumas County is over $103,000,000. A small part of this county has been covered in my book on the Mother Lode and I will only touch on those areas not covered there. I love this county for its wild rugged beauty and gold mining history. Some of the richest diggings of the Gold Rush are found here. Plumas County was created from a portion of Butte County in 1854. The name comes from El Rio de Las Plumas, which means the river of the feathers. Quincy, originally known as American Ranch, has been the only county seat. If you would like to read about everyday life in the mining camps in this area get a copy of "The Shirley Letters." The book contains a series of letters that were written by Mrs. Louise Clappe to her sister back east from Rich Bar on the Feather River. The letters are one of the best records we have telling of life in the camps during the Gold Rush.

BUTTE VALLEY

This is a very large district that runs from Lake Almanor south to the Virgilia-Twain area. It is both a placer mining and lode mining district. The district was named for an early miner and not a body part. It also includes the Seneca and Caribou areas. The placer deposits here in the Feather River and its feeder streams were very rich and this is still a good producing area. Dredgers find this a very productive area even today. Every storm seems to bring in new gold. All the tributaries to the Feather River here contain some gold for the modern prospector to find. The town of Seneca was an important mining center during the Gold Rush. The lode deposits were found early in the rush and lode mining continued into the 1930s. The gold-quartz veins are found in various rock formations but mainly in the slates and greenstone. The veins are not real rich but they are large, some as big as 20 feet thick. This district has produced a great many rich pockets as well. The placer gold deposits here are found in both the Tertiary gravels and the recent gravels and have been extremely rich in places. This is a good area for the weekend prospector and the dredger today. Go north on Highway 70 out of Oroville. It takes you right through the area.

CRESCENT MILLS

Sometimes known as the Cherokee district, Crescent Mills is the most productive gold district in the northern Sierra Nevadas. This is both a lode and placer mining area. It is located in north-central Plumas County. It is a

44

good-size district that begins around the town of Crescent Mills and goes west-northwest for 10 miles to Almanor. Production for the district is estimated anywhere from 100,000 to 250,000 ounces. The gold-quartz veins occur in granodiorite, slates, and greenstones. This is another area of rich pockets and surface ores. The veins are as thick as 20 feet and reach depths of 300 feet. A good area for the prospector to check out. Any of the creeks of this area will produce color and more. Copper is also found here. Crescent Mills is on Highway 89. Follow Highway 89 north past Greenville to the lake. They have found gold on both sides of the highway all through this area.

GENESEE

Both a placer mining and lode mining district since the early days of the Gold Rush, it is still producing small amounts of gold for the weekender. The placer gold is found in the recent gravels as well as the ancient Tertiary gravels. The lode veins are quartz. There was a large copper mine worked for quite a few years. It was named the Walker Mine and operated from 1915 to 1942. Take Road 22 off of Highway 89 to Taylorsville. Go right on the Taylorsville-Beckwourth Road to Ward Creek. This is the Genesee area. Try working the creek and you should get some color. Some of the lode mines are in the hills to the south on both sides of the creek if you are looking for one of the locations of the veins.

GRANITE BASIN

This district is shared by Plumas and Butte Counties. Other areas included in Granite Basin are the Gold Lake, Buckeye, Soapstone Mountain, Merrimac, and Milsap Bar. The placers were worked here on the north fork of the Feather River during the Gold Rush with good results. Some good-sized nuggets were found here. There was some lode mining tried here in the 1930s but it was never very rewarding. There are a few Tertiary gold bearing gravels as well as recent gold bearing gravels found here. The gold bearing veins are quartz, mainly in granite. The district is on both sides of the Butte-Plumas County line about 30 miles northeast of Oroville and 30 miles southwest of Quincy. Take Highway 70 north out of Oroville past Pulga to the county line.

JOHNSVILLE

This has been a very productive area in the past. It is both a lode and placer mining area. The placer deposits were discovered by early miners and the Plumas-Eureka mine vein was found in 1851. Instead of setting up a stamp mill at once the miners used arrastras to crush the ore from the vein. The arrastras were used until they had enough gold to purchase better equipment. These discoveries started a rush to claim up any ground that might hold a vein. The veins contained several high-grade pockets near the surface which increased the excitement and prospect holes were everywhere. The gold is in quartz veins which are not very thick but can carry as much as an ounce of gold per ton. The creeks contained quite a bit of coarse gold. Several of the mines were able to operate up into the early 1900s productively. After that, mining activity declined until the 1930s when the Depression sent people into all gold bearing areas with hopes of making enough to eat. The district is at the north end of a major belt of gold mineralization that goes south into Sierra County. Production for the district is estimated at as high as $20,000,000. Part of the district is included in the Plumas-Eureka State Park. This is somewhat of an overlooked area considering the rich placer deposits that were worked in the early days. The Plumas-Eureka Mine was one of the first veins discovered and one of the richest. The mine is now part of the state park. There is a nice museum in the former mine bunkhouse and office that con-

46

tains not only displays from the mining days but also Indian and natural history displays. Take Road A14 (Graeagle-Johnsville Road) from Highway 70-89 to reach the area.

LA PORTE

This is one of the most productive placer gold mining regions in California. The 49'ers flocked to this area during the rush because of the richness of the deposits. The original site was located on flat benches on both sides of Rabbit Creek. It was like a scene from a movie with men digging everywhere and finding gold. La Porte was first known as Rabbit Creek or Rabbit Town but the name was changed to La Porte in 1857. I love the original names given to the camps like Hangtown, Drunken Gulch, Whiskey Flats, Poverty Bar, and others. Respectability kinda takes the charm away, doesn't it? To give you an idea of the richness of the area, production for the years 1853 to 1871 is set at over $80,000,000 at the old price of gold. This is primarily a placer mining district but there has been some lode and drift mining done here. Some fairly large scale mining was done here from the days of the Gold Rush right up to the Second World War. The gold mostly comes from the ancient Tertiary channel gravels of the North Fork of the Yuba River known as the La Porte channel. The channel runs from Gibsonville to the north into this region and continues south where it is joined by a channel from the east which comes from the St. Louis-Table Rock area. Here at La Porte the channel is from 300 to 1500 feet wide and as much as 500 feet thick. The quartz-rich lower gravels are 80-feet thick and contain varying amounts of gold. The richest gravels are on or near bedrock and in the early days contained as much as an ounce of gold per yard of material. The district is in the southwestern part of the county about 25-30 miles south of Quincy. Take Highway 20 east off of Highway 70 in Marysville to Road E21. This is also called La Porte Road. This will take you to La Porte.

LIGHT'S CANYON

This is mainly a placer gold area but some lode mining has also been done here. As in most districts the placer deposits were first discovered during the Gold Rush. Both the Tertiary and recent gravels contained fair amounts of gold. The lode deposits are gold-quartz veins which are not very wide but have been very rich in places. This district is in northeastern Plumas County and includes the Kettle Rock area to the east, and the Moonlight Valley area to the west, as well as the Indian Valley area. Copper mining has been very successful at the Engel's Mine as well as others. You might do well to check for copper ore as well as gold here. Lights Creek joins Indian Creek about four miles from Taylorsville. Take the Diamond Mountain Road out of Taylorsville to reach the area.

MEADOWS VALLEY

Meadows Valley has produced a fair amount of gold from the Tertiary gravels found around Spanish Ranch and the ancient lake gravels contain small amounts of gold in some areas. There has been little lode mining done here except at one mine called the Diaden. The district is in west central Plumas County about eight miles from Quincy and runs from Spanish Ranch to Bucks Lake. It includes The Spanish Peak and Edmanton areas as well as Spanish Ranch and Bucks Lake areas. Little work has been done here since the early 1900s. Take Highway 70 west from Quincy to reach the region.

MOOREVILLE RIDGE

This district is also in Butte County and most of the gold was mined by hydraulicking. A lot of dredgers like this area because it is remote and not overworked like a lot of other areas. It includes the Camel Peak and American

House areas. The gold is in the recent gravels and in the Tertiary channel gravels that run through here. Portions of the south fork of the Feather River here were mined in the early days. The district is southwest of Plumas County. This is a good dredging area but remote and hard to get to. Take the Mooreville Ridge Road off of the La Porte Road at Clipper Mills.

QUINCY

This is the county seat as well as a productive gold mining area. The placers were first worked during the Gold Rush and mining has gone on in this district on and off ever since. Most of the placer gold has come from the Tertiary gravels in the southern portion of the district but the recent gravels also contain gold so don't overlook them. Lode mining first began here in the 1850s. The veins are gold-quartz found mainly in slate and mica schist and can be as thick as 15 feet. This district also includes the Butterfly Valley and Elizabethtown areas. The area can be reached by taking Highway 70 or 89.

RICH BAR

This is one of my favorite places to work, not because of how much gold I get but because after reading the *Shirley Letters* you feel like you're returning in time to the Gold Rush era. When you first look down at this area from the road, you wonder where you could put thousands of miners and a camp and you remember her description of her first view of "Barra Rica," as the Mexican miners called it. She wrote, "Imagine a tiny valley about 800 yards in length and perhaps 30 in width . . . through the middle of Rich Bar runs the street, thickly planted with about 40 tenements, among which figure round tents, square tents, plank hovels, log cabins etc.—the residences varying in splendor from 'the Empire' (a hotel) down to local

Jon and Andy Klein panning a creek in Northern California.

habitation formed of pine boughs and covered with old calico shirts." The deposits were discovered in July of 1850 by miners who had rushed to Gold Lake and, when that fizzled, worked their way around the area looking for good diggings in places like Onion Valley and Nelson's Point. Well, they found it here. The early miners' pans of dirt sometimes held from $100 to $1000 worth of gold. Three German miners are reported to have taken out $36,000 in nuggets and dust in just four days. Claims were so rich that they were limited to 10 square feet. The first two years over $4,000,000 in gold was taken out of this small area. Rich Bar was worked so hard by the first miners that the deposits were quickly depleted and by 1852 it was already a ghost town. Nothing remains of Rich Bar today to let you know that this was once a rip-roaring mining camp. When you visit the area it is easy to see how the mighty Feather River could reclaim it for herself. Work the gravel bars on both sides of the bridge for placer gold and look for narrow gold-quartz veins for the lode deposits. Rich Bar is on Highway 70 north out of Oroville and a few miles past Belden.

SAWPIT FLAT

This is a large gold bearing region that includes the Harrison Flat, Monitor Flat, Onion Valley, Last Chance, Blue Nose Mountain, Nelson Point, and Sawpit Flat areas. It is located in southern Plumas County and runs from the Quincy district to the north to the Gibsonville district in Sierra County to the south. The placer gold is found in Tertiary and recent gravels. The Tertiary gravels contain large amounts of quartz and have been very rich in places. There are quite a few gold-quartz veins that have been mined here. Large scale mining was done here from the early days of the Gold Rush right up to the turn-of-the-century and some form of mining has gone on right up to today. Try your luck on the Middle Fork of the

Feather River and Monitor Flat area. Both have been productive recently. Other streams in the area have produced some good gold so don't overlook them. The district starts about five miles south of Quincy and runs south to the Gibsonville district in Sierra County. Take the La Porte-Quincy road to reach this area.

SPRING GARDEN

Spring Garden is a small district in the southcentral part of the county and has been both placer mined and lode mined. A small amount of Tertiary channel gravels are found here as well as a few small gold-quartz veins. Spring Garden is about 10 miles south of Quincy on Highway 70-89. Take Greenhorn Ranch Road east and work the creek for a little color.

TAYLORSVILLE

The Taylorsville district has not been as productive as the districts around it such as Lights Canyon and Genesee Valley but a fair amount of gold has been mined here. The placers were first mined in the Gold Rush and lode mining followed soon after. The gold-quartz veins are narrow and usually occur in granodiorite or near it. Take Road 207 off of Highway 89 after its junction with Highway 70 to reach Taylorsville.

TREASURE TALES

There are several tales told about lost gold mines, ledges, and rich creek deposits in Plumas County. Probably the granddaddy of all the lost treasure stories from the Gold Rush is Stoddard's Lost Lake of Gold. Stoddard claimed that he stumbled upon a lake in the higher mountains somewhere between Downieville and Sierra Valley. He said the shores of the lake were covered with chunks of gold. At that time in the Gold Rush the wildest

52

extravaganza seemed believable to the gold-seekers and they were all certain that the great bonanza or the "Mother Lode" was just around the corner. So it isn't surprising that a large group of miners formed a search party to look for the Lost Lake of Gold. They set off with Stoddard leading them and wandered all over the mountains finding nothing. After weeks of searching, the miners were getting mighty unhappy with Stoddard. When he heard the miners talking about a lynching one night, he took off as fast as he could and disappeared. This was not the only group that was searching for the gold lake. It is estimated that at least 1,000 miners left their diggings to hunt for Stoddard's Lake. There is a Gold Lake but don't go there hoping to pick up nuggets off the shore because you will be disappointed.

Another popular treasure tale that is more likely to be worthwhile searching for is Lost Gordier Treasure. Gordier was a successful miner from the Gold Rush who used his earnings from mining to buy a farm and some cattle. He was active in the community and when no one saw him for a spell, some of his neighbors decided to check on him. They found several rough looking men living in his cabin. They claimed that they had bought the cabin from Gordier and that he had returned to France. Gordier's body was found several days later in Willow Creek. He had been murdered and his body weighted down and dumped into the creek. The local men got together and went to Gordier's cabin and arrested the men there. After a quick trial the men were found guilty and hung. Everyone knew that Gordier had quite a bit of gold and guessed that he had buried it some- place on his property like everyone else did in those days. There were holes all around the place but the men claimed they never found the cache of gold. It is thought that there would be at least $40,000 in the cache. At today's prices for gold it would be well worth looking for. The farm was on Baxter Creek north of Honey Lake.

HISTORICAL SITES

Many of the districts listed here are historical sites from the Gold Rush and worth visiting. There are some other interesting places such as the site of Peter Lassen's Trading Post, which is four and a half miles east of Greenville on the Beckwourth-Greenville Road, and the Pioneer Grave, three miles southwest of Buck's Ranch. The grave is that of a young man who was murdered in 1852 for his gold dust.

SHASTA COUNTY

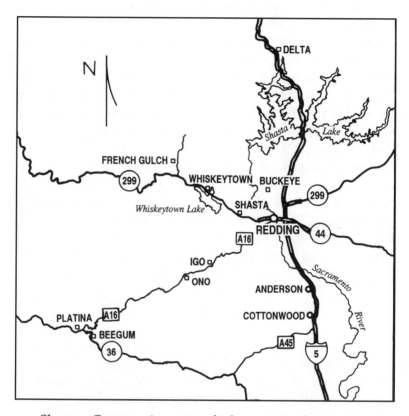

Shasta County is one of the original counties in California. It originally contained all the territory that is now Lassen and Modoc Counties and portions of the present Plumas, Siskiyou, and Tehama Counties. The name Shasta is thought to be a corruption of the name of a tribe of Indians that lived around Mount Shasta. The first county seat was at Reading's Ranch, then moved to Shasta in 1851, and finally to Redding in 1888. Gold was first found here by pioneer P.B. Reading in 1848. Reading had worked at Sutter's Fort in 1844 and through Sutter's influence received a land grant of 26,000 acres, the most northernly grant in California. In February of 1848, Reading was one of the first to visit the spot of Marshall's discovery of gold at Sutter's Mill. After looking at the land there he was convinced that there must be gold on his own ranch and he quickly returned to investigate. In March, Reading and some Indians washed out the first gold to be found in Shasta County. This was at the mouth of Clear Creek at what became known as Reading's Bar. In July he made the discovery of gold on the Trinity River. Shasta County is the location of one of my favorite prospecting areas, French Gulch. This county has also had a copper rush. Around the turn of the century there was a real copper mining boom here. By 1906 there were six copper smelters running here. There was a problem with sulfur fumes killing the vegetation around the smelters, causing most to close. This is good place for weekend prospectors. Shasta County is credited with production of over 2,000,000 ounces of gold with one-quarter of the gold coming from the placer deposits.

BACKBONE

This district is located about 10 miles north of Redding. It is bordered by the French Gulch district and includes the Squaw Creek area. This is mainly a lode gold district with little or no placer production. The Uncle Sam was the largest producer with recorded production of over $1,000,000. This district is in the main copper belt of Shasta County. Most all the mining has been for the gold. The veins are gold-quartz and are not large in most cases. The Backbone area is on the west side of Shasta Lake between the lake and Shasta Lake Road.

COTTONWOOD

This was a very rich placer mining district in the early days and gold is still found here. Cottonwood Creek is the boundary line for Shasta and Tehama Counties. This district also includes the Gas Point area. Cottonwood Creek

56

is a feeder creek to the upper Sacramento River. Its tributaries such as Antelope Creek, Dry Creek, and Crow Creek have also been productive. During the Depression the area was dredged by bucket line dredging. Cottonwood Creek crosses Highway 5 south of the town of Cottonwood.

DOG CREEK

This is a small district in northwestern Shasta County. Some placer mining was done here in the early days and lode gold mining began in the late 1800s. Most of the creeks in this area will produce a little color. This is also known as the Delta District. The veins are narrow, low grade gold-quartz but they extend for a good distance. Dog Creek crosses Highway 5 about 25 miles north of Redding right before you get to the town of Delta. The main part of Dog Creek is west of the highway.

Jon Klein setting up a sluice in Shasta County.

FRENCH GULCH

This is an excellent area for the weekend prospector. Not only is it a good placer mining area, it is the most important lode mining district in the Klamath Mountains. Production for this district is over $50,000,000. The placer deposits were discovered in 1849 by French Miners. It was originally called Morrowville but the name was soon changed to French Gulch. The district runs along the Shasta-Trinity County line but is put into Shasta County. The Deadwood area is also included in this district. Clear Creek is the main placering area. I found that the cemented red gravels were good. You have to break off the material from the banks to wash, but the material will break down in your pan. The gold-quartz veins can be several feet thick and have contained some rich pockets in places. During the rush the miners even tore down their cabins to work the vein when it ran underneath the cabin. Go west from Redding on Highway 299 to Trinity Mountain Road. Turn right (north) and follow this road a few miles to the power station on your right. You can work Clear Creek here and most always at least get some color.

Jon Klein working in French Gulch District.

58

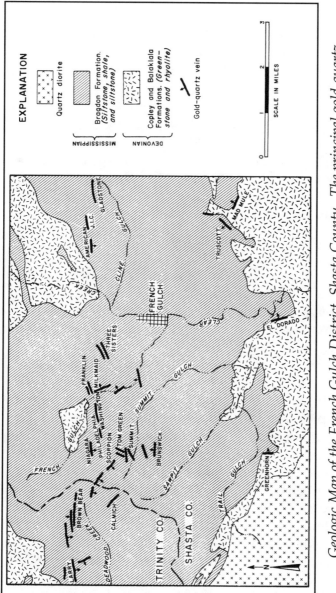

Geologic Map of the French Gulch District, Shasta County. The principal gold-quartz veins are shown. (Reprinted, by permission, from California Division of Mines and Geology. *Gold Districts of California, 137*)

HARRISON GULCH

Some placering was done here early but the main discovery didn't occur until the 1890s. The Midas Mine vein was uncovered in 1894 and became one of the major mines of the Klamath Mountains. Most of the production for the district has come from that mine. Placer gold has been found in Harrison Gulch and in the Beegum Creek and Platina areas nearby. The district is located in the southwest portion of the county. The gold-quartz veins are found in greenstone and schist. The veins are from one to three feet wide. Take Gas Point Road west to Platina Road and turn left. This will take you into the area.

IGO-ONO

This is actually two districts; the Igo and the Ono areas. This is mainly a placer mining area. The placers were first worked in the Gold Rush. Later the deposits were worked by hydraulic and drift mining. The Chinese miners were also busy here. The placers here have produced several hundred thousand ounces of gold. There are several different stories on how the districts got their names. One says that a preacher named Kidder named Ono from the Bible's "plains of Ono." The one I like best is that the name came from one of the miners and his young son. According to the story, every morning when the miner would leave to work his son would ask, "I go" and his dad would answer "O no, not today." The district is credited with over 200,000 ounces of gold produced from the placer deposits. The gold is found in the recent stream gravels and the bench deposits and has been recovered from Dry Creek, Clear Creek, Eagle Creek, North Cottonwood, and South Fork. The gold-quartz veins are small but contain some rich pockets. The district is located in southwestern Shasta County about 15 miles from Redding. Take A-16 (Placer Road) west out of Redding to Platina Road and go west to this area. Platina Road crosses Eagle Creek near the site of Ono.

OLD DIGGINGS

Estimated production for this district is 300,000 ounces of gold. This is both a placer mining and lode mining area. The placers were first worked in the Gold Rush and were very productive. This is also known as the Buckeye District because the first miners here were from Ohio. The ore here is very pretty white sugar quartz and the veins range from a few feet thick to as much as 25 feet thick. This district has produced several high-grade pockets in the past. The placer gold is found in the recent gravels as well as in the terrace deposits. The terrace gravels can be very productive and produced large amounts of gold when they were hydraulicked in the early days. Buckeye is located about five miles north of Redding on Road A-18 (Lake Boulevard) and the Walker Mine Road meets A-18 above Buckeye going west.

REDDING

This district is located on part of Major Reading's original land grant but is named for Ben Redding who was a land agent for the railroad. Quite a bit of gold has come from placer mining on the Sacramento River, Clear Creek, Oregon Creek, and Flat Creek. Major Reading made the first discovery of gold in Shasta County in March of 1848 on Clear Creek. There were some rich surface pockets found here as well. The gold-quartz veins are not very big but they do contain some very rich pockets in places. Redding is a nice-sized town and a good place to stock up your supplies if you're camping out like me. You can also get some food not cooked by yourself over a campfire for a change of pace. Redding is located on Highway 5 and Clear Creek crosses the highway a few miles south of the town.

SHASTA

There are two gold districts with Shasta in their name. There is the one most people think of when talking about gold and prospecting which is the Shasta-Whiskeytown area, but there is also the Shasta copper-zinc belt district that has also produced a great deal of gold. In the Shasta copper-zinc belt region it was gold that first brought the miners to the area and they were successful with several mines being worked at one time. In the 1890s the copper veins were developed and were very productive for the next thirty years. Quite a bit of gold was also recovered as a by-product of the copper-zinc mining during this period. Gold production is set at over .5 million ounces for this district. The gold-quartz veins in this area are found in slate and greenstone. The Shasta copper-zinc belt is located in the Klamath Mountain foothills a few miles of Redding. Some of this area is now under Shasta Lake. The Shasta-Whiskeytown District is located about 10 miles west and north of Redding. The placer deposits were worked early, and Whiskeytown was settled in 1849 by miners in the Gold Rush. The post office refused to allow the name until 1952. Until then the post office had been called Blair, then Stella and, lastly, Schelling. The old town is under Whiskeytown Lake now and the present Whiskeytown was established later. The French Gulch district is on the west side of this district. The Clear Creek placer deposits were the first to be discovered and the Whiskey Creek and others shortly after that. Other areas in this district include Horse Town and Shasta City. Horse Town got its name from a prospector who arrived there with a lone pack animal and said, "This is sure a one-horse town alright." After that the name of the camp became One Horse Town. The remains of Shasta City are some of the most interesting in northern California. This is mainly a placer mining district but there are some gold quartz veins. The gold quartz veins are found mainly in granite or greenstone and schist.

Go west on Highway 299 and it will take you right to the area. To do any panning inside the Whiskeytown recreation area you have to register at the Information Center and get a set of rules and regulations for mining there.

TREASURE TALES

There are several tales of lost mines and buried bandit loot told here. One is the story told of the Ruggles gang who robbed a stagecoach a few miles north of Redding in an area known as Blue Cut. When the Ruggles stopped the stage a gunfight broke out and one of the Ruggles, a stage guard, and the driver were wounded. The strong box was taken from the stage by the robbers and emptied of its gold. The stage guard died when the coach got to Redding. Charles Ruggles, the wounded bandit, was found hiding in some bushes by a posse, and John Ruggles was captured a month later. Both men were hanged and refused to tell were they had hidden the loot. Most people guess that it is buried somewhere near Blue Cut and marked by some kind of monument.

There is also said to be a bag of gold hidden in a cave in a pool of water somewhere along Beegum Creek. The gold belonged to two miners who were attacked and killed by marauding Indians who hid the gold before being captured. The Indians would only tell their captors what they had done with the gold but not where it was.

Another cave treasure story is told about Bear Creek. A lone prospector found the small cave entrance and decided to check it out. When he got inside he found a large room filled with gold and other items and made off with all he could carry. After a spree in Redding he returned to Bear Creek but couldn't find the entrance again. He had hidden it so well even he couldn't tell where it was.

A miner working Cow Creek found a rich gold-quartz ledge exposed near the head of the creek. He filled two sacks full of the rich ore and hid the outcropping. He sold the ore in Redding and stocked up on provisions and returned to work the ledge. When he got to the area he became confused and couldn't find the rich ledge of gold again. It's still there waiting for some lucky prospector to find.

HISTORICAL SITES

The Old Town of Shasta is worth stopping at. It is located on Highway 299 about six miles west of Redding. First called Reading's Spring it was changed to Shasta in 1850. At one time this was the most important city in upper northern California. Look up on the hills behind the ruins along the highway for more interesting ruins.

Reading's Bar is located about three and half miles east of Igo off Clear Creek Road. It is the site of the first gold discovery in Shasta County.

Fort Reading was established in 1852 to protect the miners and settlers. It was the first and largest U.S. Army fort in northern California. It was abandoned in 1867. The site is six miles northeast of Anderson.

James Klein at Reading's Bar.

Rules & Regulations in the Early Days

From the beginning of the Gold Rush, the need for some laws or agreements that would regulate the ownership of mining claims was apparent. There was no well-developed American Mining code in 1848, but in Europe, South America and Mexico a body of ordinances had evolved through centuries of experience in regulating mining practices. It was these ordinances, adapted to the New World and introduced primarily by English and Latin American gold-seekers, that provided the basis for California mining law.

The usual procedure, in setting up laws, was for each camp or each local territorial unit (such as a gulch or section of river), to hold an open meeting for all the miners working there. At this meeting, the camp or area would be formally declared a mining district and a set of regulations would be drawn up governing all claims within that area. The districts were not of a standard size or shape. They were political units which simply coalesced about the most convenient assembly places and conformed to purely physical boundaries. The boundaries were drawn to include not only the claims of all the miners present, but also all the unclaimed ground that was reasonably accessible and likely to be valuable. The discovery of new mines might at any time create new camps, but not necessarily new districts, unless the miners involved assembled, made new regulations, and separated themselves from the jurisdiction of their former regulations.

Although specific details of the regulations varied between districts, the fundamental principles were the same. . .that the man who discovered a section of gold-bearing ground had the right to exploit it, and that this right lasted only so long as he continued to work his claim. Each man could locate or "claim," only one section of ground, but he could purchase the claims of others and the discoverer of a new district was customarily allowed to hold up to twice as much land as a person who arrived later. In addition, every code stipulated the maximum allowable size of a claim in the district, as well as the manner in which claim boundaries were to be marked. Wells, referring to the discovery of gold on Yreka Flats by Abraham Thompson in March, 1851, writes:

> *The men were nearly all new arrivals in the mines and were ignorant of mining methods and customs but two or three who had been in the mines told them they must organize a district and make regulations. A meeting was therefore held the next day. The new diggings were called Thompson's Dry Diggings, and the size of the claim was made thirty feet, the later action being taken in deference to the superior wisdom of the favored few who had been in the mines and knew all about it, though they afterward learned that they could have made them much larger. Thompson and his partner, Bell, were given three claims the extra for the discovery.*

One by one, the mining districts formed and established codes. An example of one of these is the following from the Liberty District (Salmon River area) in what was at that time Klamath County:

> *At a meeting of the miners of Liberty Township, County of Klamath in the State of California, the following laws were adopted on this the 15th day of May A.D. 1860.*

THIS MINING DISTRICT SHALL INCLUDE ALL THE GOLD MINES IN THIS TOWNSHIP.

Article 1st

A bar or bank claim for mining purposes on the river shall be one hundred feet in length and extend back to the base of the mountain.

Article 2nd

Each and every man within the bounds of this district shall perform actual labor upon such claims one day out of every six or employ substitutes to perform such labor otherwise such claim shall be forfeited, Provided that wet claims and claims not workable in the rainy season shall be good without work being performed from the 15th of November to the 15th of May, Provided that said claim be noticed and recorded. This Article not to take effect until the 1st day of July 1860.

Article 3rd

A claim in the gulches or ravines shall be one hundred yards in length and extend to the base of the mountain on each side of the claim and shall be worked one day in every six when workable. Eddy Gulch and Jack Ass Gulch excepted.

Article 4th

A Quartz claim in this district shall be 200 feet in length and shall be subject to the same laws as other gold mines in this district.

Article 5th

In case of sickness no miner shall forfeit his claim.

Article 6th

All claims which are or shall be located to be worked at any future time shall be recorded in a book kept by a Recorder for that purpose and all claims so located upon any bar or in any gulch or in the bed of the river shall be worked once in six days when workable.

Article 7th

The Recorder shall receive fifty cents for recording each claim.

Article 8th

Any man or company of men discovering new mining localities shall be entitled to one claim extra.

Article 9th

All claims now located shall stand as they now are.

Article 10th

Any river claimed hereafter located shall be one hundred feet in length and extend to low water mark on each side of the river and all river claims small be considered workable on the first day of July. It shall be considered low water at any time the water is turned from its natural channel.

Article 11th

Any person having a bank claim and a river claim may leave his bank claim to work in the river and said bank claim shall not be jumpable during such time as a miner may be to work in the river.

Article 12th

The foregoing laws or any part of them may be amended or repealed in the following manner. On the written application of ten miners to the Recorder he shall post notices in the different localities in this district giving at least ten day's notice of a meeting to be held for said purpose. A two thirds vote of the miners present shall be required to amend or repeal. No amendment under this article shall cut down or diminish the size of claims.

Article 13th

There shall be a Recorder elected at this meeting and annually thereafter who shall hold his office for one year or until his successor is elected and qualified. In case the recorder leaves he shall give at least twenty days notice beforehand. Passed May 27th, 1860.

For decades, locally developed regulations such as these helped to maintain order in what could have been chaotic situations. The regulations gradually came to be enforced by the courts of the state, and in 1866 were sanctioned by federal law. This law (originally applicable only to lode claims), established:

First - That all the mineral lands of the public domain shall be free and open to exploration and occupation;

Second - That rights which had been acquired in these lands under a system of local rule, with the apparent acquiescence and sanction of the government, shall be recognized and confirmed:

Third - That titles to at least certain classes of mineral deposits on lands containing them might be ultimately obtained.

In 1870, the Placer Act extended the provision of this law to placer claims, and two years later, the Acts of 1866 and 1870 were repassed by Congress as a single statute entitled "The United States Mining Law of 1872."

With minor exceptions, this law still governs the acquisition of mining rights on federally owned land.

SISKIYOU COUNTY

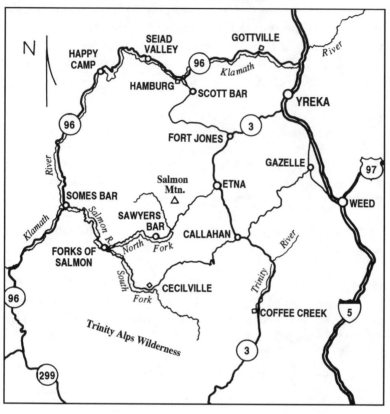

The Klamath River region is one of the most popular areas for dredgers today. I know prospectors who live in southern California and have claims on the Klamath that they travel to several times a year. They all say that the gold you get here makes it well worth the trip. Siskiyou County was created in 1852 from parts of Shasta County and the old Klamath County. Yreka has always been the county seat. The name Siskiyou is thought to be a Cree Indian word for "bobtailed horse." A trapper is said to have lost a horse in the area in 1828 and the name came from that incident. The first gold seekers from Oregon passed through the region on their way to the gold fields of the Sierra Nevada without stopping to prospect the area. That's why they called it a Gold Rush; people rushed to the Mother Lode country without stopping for anything. It is thought that no mining was done here before 1850 but I think the miners were working here before then. In June of 1850 miners did explore the rugged Salmon Mountains. They crossed the ridge from the North Fork of the Trinity River to the South Fork of the Salmon River and followed that river to the North Fork where they found rich placer deposits. This camp became known as the Forks of the Salmon. About the same time miners began searching the Klamath River from its mouth to the Shasta River. They found gold almost everywhere along the river and other miners soon followed. The placer deposits at Yreka were discovered by miners leaving the Klamath River for the warmer climate of the Sacramento Valley that winter. The Yreka discovery was overshadowed by the discovery of rich diggings at Ingall's Gulch on Greenhorn Creek. This is beautiful country and there are still a lot of unspoiled areas to visit here. Siskiyou County is in the top dozen gold producing counties in the state with estimated production set at over $100,000,000.

CALLAHAN

This is mainly a placer mining district but some good lode mining has been done here as well. The first miners worked the stream gravels and then the bench deposits which were very productive. The gulch's tributary to the Scott River have been very good. The Scott River here was worked by bucket line dredges in the early 1900s and the 1930s. The veins are gold-quartz in granite. The veins are narrow but sometimes very rich. The district is located in south-central Siskiyou County. To reach Callahan take the Gazelle-Callahan Road south and west out of the town of Gazelle. Gazelle is located between Yreka and Weed.

Placer Mine, Siskiyou County. Water wheel and flume appear in this view of a mine operated by Chinese miners on the Klamath River in 1933. At one time, these Chinese water wheels were widely used in river mining.
(Courtesy of Olaf P. Jenkins)

CECILVILLE

This is both a lode mining and placer mining district in southwestern Siskiyou County. The placers were discovered early in the Gold Rush and soon there were several thousand miners working in the area. This is another area where, later on, the Chinese miners found more gold working the gravels left over by the first miners then the original miners did. There have been several good lode mines worked here. The gold-quartz veins are quite large in some places. There have been some rich pockets also found here in the past. Cecilville is located near the junction of the east and south forks of the Salmon River. Take the Callahan-Cecilville Road out of the town of Callahan to reach Cecilville.

DEADWOOD

This was a very rich placer mining area during the Gold Rush. Most every creek in the region produced large amounts of gold. Deadwood Creek, Indian Creek, French Creek, Cherry Creek, and McAdam Creek were especially productive. Some of the lode mines have produced good results in the past. The gold-quartz veins are found mostly in greenstone and, though not huge, are productive. Take Highway 3 west out of Yreka to Greenhorn Road and go north on Greenhorn into this area. Greenhorn Road crosses Cherry Creek.

DILLON CREEK

This area has the honor of having one of the modern day gold mine discoveries and developments. The Siskon Mine vein was discovered in 1951 and produced several million dollars in gold for its owner. The placer deposits were discovered during the Gold Rush and were quite good. Dillon Creek is a tributary to the Klamath River and is located in the western part of the county. Both the recent stream gravels and the bench deposits were productive. Take Highway 96 southwest out of Happy Camp to reach this area. It is right before Persido Bar.

DORLESKA

Dorleska is a lode mining district in the Salmon Mountains. The district is shared by both Siskiyou and Trinity Counties. The veins were first worked in any great way in the 1890s. The gold-quartz veins are not large but contain some high-grade pockets. The district is located near the head of Coffee Creek. This is in the Trinity Alps Wilderness region but there is a rough road (Coffee Creek Road) into the area from Highway 3 north of Carrville. Carrville is in the north part of the Whiskeytown Recreation Area.

GAZELLE

This is another small lode gold mining area. The veins were first worked in the 1880s and mining lasted until after the turn of the century. Since then there has been little activity here. The gold-quartz veins occur in granodiorite. The district is located in the southcentral portion of the county. Take Highway 5 north out of Weed to reach Gazelle. The area is to west of the town.

GILTA

Quite a bit of gold came out of this area in the early days and you can still get some color out of the creek here. This is both a lode gold mining and placer mining area. The placer deposits in Knownothing Creek were very rich. The gold is found in the recent stream gravels and bank deposits. The veins are gold-quartz found in slate and schist. The district is located in the southwestern part of the county. To reach this area take the Somes Bar-Etna Road west off of Highway 3 at Etna and go to Forks of the Salmon and turn left on South Forks of the Salmon Road. Knownothing Creek crosses the road a few miles south of the junction.

HUMBUG

There are several Humbugs in California. It was a popular term given to an area that didn't pan out. This one is in the central portion of the county 10 miles north of Yreka. The placer deposits were discovered in May of 1851, by a party of miners who were told to turn back because the reports of gold in the area "were just a bunch of humbug." Humbug City was quite a busy camp during the early days. It was said to be a rough place and as wild as the mountains that hemmed it in. It was also said to be out of sight of everything. The placers on Humbug Creek are said to have produced over $15,000,000 in gold. The gold is found in the recent stream gravels. There have also been some gold-quartz veins worked here with good results. The veins range in size from one to five feet thick and several rich pockets have been found. To reach this area go north on Highway 5 to Highway 96, go west on Highway 96 to Humbug Creek road. This road will take you into the region.

KLAMATH RIVER

A lot of former separate gold districts such as Happy Camp, Greenhorn, Hornbrook, Cottonwood, Fool's Paradise, Gottville, Hamburg, Indian Creek, Oak Bar, Seiad, Somes Bar, and Yreka are now included in this district. Each of those districts really deserve to be classified separately and not bunched into one unit. For example the city of Yreka sits on the site of what was very rich diggings–at one time. Where Yama and Discovery Streets meet in the city was the location of Yreka Flats where gold was discovered in 1851. More than 2,000 men rushed to the area in six weeks time and a camp sprang that was first called Thompson's Dry Diggings. The name was changed soon after to Yreka. Yreka was also the location of the Greenhorn War in 1855. The war erupted over water rights on Greenhorn Creek and even had the miners on lower Greenhorn Creek marching on the jail and freeing a prisoner who had violated a court order about the water rights. The gold is found in the present stream gravels and bench and terrace deposits and has been very rich in places. Most of the tributaries to the Klamath River have been gold bearing. A lot of this area is claimed up but there are a lot of areas where you can still work. Creeks feeding the river such as Humbug Creek, Empire Creek, Dutch Creek, Willow Creek, Bogus Creek, Lumgrey Creek, Indian Creek, China Creek, and many others, have all produced gold in various amounts. You can really try just about anywhere along the river and surrounding areas and should get gold. The Scotts River is also a good spot where it joins the Klamath and south of the junction. There have been several lode gold mining areas included in the Klamath River district, such as around Gottville. Take Highway 96 west off of Highway 5 and follow the river. There is more than 60 miles along the river to search. Take Hornbrook-Copco Road east off of Highway 5 north of Yreka to reach that portion of the Klamath River. There was a lot of gold to come out of that area from Bogus Creek.

LIBERTY

This is a small lode gold and placer gold mining area. The placer deposits were first worked in the Gold Rush and the lode deposits soon after that. This is sometimes called the Black Bear district after the Black Bear Mine found here. It is located about 10 miles east of the Forks of the Salmon. The gold-quartz veins are from one to five feet thick with some rich pockets. Eddys Gulch Road out of Sawyers Bar will take you into the area.

Miners are shown bringing an ore cart out of the
Black Bear adit. Above are some of the dumps of the mine
which show the large amount of rock removed
from underground. The photo was taken about 1900.
(Reprinted, by permission, from Siskiyou County Historical Society,
The Siskiyou Pioneer, 24)

ORO FINO

This is a small lode gold and placer gold mining area. The placers were found early in the Gold Rush and the first miners during that period were lucky and hit some rich deposits in several of the gulches and creeks here. This district also includes the Mugginsville and Quartz Valley areas. After the placers were worked out the miners began looking for the source of the placer deposits and discovered the veins on Quartz Hill. The placer deposits are in the recent stream gravels. Some nice coarse gold nuggets have been found here. The veins are quartz-calcite often in diorite. The veins have been worked off and on from the Gold Rush to recent times. The quartz is white or smoky-white in color. The district is in the central part of the county near Fort Jones. Take the Oro Fino Road west off of Highway 3 south of Fort Jones to reach this area.

SALMON RIVER

The Salmon River has produced a lot of gold over the years. This is mainly a placer mining district with the gold being found in the stream gravels and in the bench deposits but there have been some lode deposits worked here as well. The first miners that flocked to the area suffered greatly. Only about 50 of the most hardy of the several hundred miners who were working there tried to ride out the first winter in 1850. Early in 1851, when word of the rich diggings got out, more and more miners rushed to the area and when late snows blocked the trails in March, the poorly equipped miners almost starved to death. The most productive districts have been at Sawyers Bar, Snowden, Cecilville, Forks of the Salmon, and Knownothing. Sawyers Bar on the North Fork of the Salmon River has suffered a great deal from fires like a lot of camps. The only building which survived every fire was St. Joseph's Catholic Church. Is that the hand of God showing? Probably, I'd say. Early estimates say that the area between Sawyer's Bar and Forks of the Salmon produced $25,000,000 alone. The Salmon River drains the Salmon Mountains in the central part of the county. Take Highway 96 south from Happy Camp to Somes Bar-Etna Road, this road will take you along the river. Somes Bar is the first camp site on the river from its mouth.

SCOTT'S BAR

Scott's Bar is named for John Scott who first worked the placer deposits here in 1850. The original Scott's was a few hundred feet above and on the opposite bank of the Scott River from the later Scott's Bar. The old trail of the 1850s ran three miles through the steep canyon from the mouth of the river and Scott's Bar. At places the rugged canyon is at least 3,000 feet deep. At one time there were camps all along the great gorge. Some of the camps were French Bar, Poorman's Bar, Slapjack Bar, Michigan Bar, and others. This is mainly a placer mining area but there has been a small amount of lode gold mining done as well. The placer gold is found in the recent stream gravels and in the bench deposits. The veins are gold in quartz-calcite and found in schist. There have been some rich pockets found here. Take Scott's Bar Road south off of Highway 96 right before Hamburg to reach this area.

ROCK AND GEM SITES

There has been some jade found in Siskiyou County as well as some good serpentine and garnet. One location is near Happy Camp. To reach the collecting area take Indian Creek Road out of Happy Camp to the west branch of Indian Creek, it's about 13 miles. Search on the left hand side of the creek. You can try most of the creeks here as gemstones occurred at various places.

West Miner Street in Yreka, taken from an 1851 or 1852 daguerreotype.
(Reprinted, by permission, from Siskiyou County Historical Society, *Gold Mining in Siskiyou County 1850-1900*, 90)

TREASURE TALES

There is a story told of a hidden cache of gold on the McCloud River about seven miles east of the town of McCloud. According to the story, five miners were working a rich ledge of gold there. Worried about robbers and Indian raiders, the men buried all the gold they recovered each day. They had been working for several weeks when they were attacked by Indians and four of the miners were killed, but one managed to escape. He was able to reach the camp and safety after a day or so. He was afraid to go back for the gold because he feared the Indians would kill him. Several months went by before he got up the courage to return. When he did return he found that everything had changed and he couldn't locate the spot again. He said it was still out there waiting for some lucky treasure hunter to find. One clue we know of was that there was a waterfall near the campsite.

Another tale has it that a stage coach was held up near the town of Weed and two strongboxes carrying $50 gold coins worth over $100,000 were taken. The sheriff and a posse seeking another robber found the stage, heard what had happened and set out after the bandits. They caught up with them a short time later, a gunfight broke out, and the bandits were all killed. The saddlebags on the robbers horses were empty so they must have hidden the loot before the sheriff found them. The posse searched for the gold coins but never found them. They think the coins were buried somewhere on the slopes of Mt. Shasta.

HISTORICAL SITES

You can get a feel of the early days by visiting the "West Miner Street-Third Street Historic District Area" in Yreka. It dates from 1854 and includes both commercial and residential buildings.

Lava Beds National Monument contains several historic spots including "Captain Jack's Stronghold," Guillen's Graveyard, and Canby's Cross.

VALUE OF THE KLAMATH RIVER MINES
1872-1885

By the Late H.J. Barton

The following is an estimate of productivity, recorded by H. J. Barton of Oak Bar, of the area along the Klamath River, from Humbug to Scott River. Owners of the following properties measured the length, width and depth and approximate amount of gold taken from each claim, as worked by the owners. From 621,834 cubic yards there was taken $866,158, or an average of one dollar and thirty-nine cents ($1.39) per cubic yard.

	Size of Ground Worked				Value	Average
	Length	Width	No. Cu. Depth	Taken yds	per Out	YD.
Kanaka, P.M - Freshour's ranch,						
Virginia Bar	100 ft.	50 ft.	10 ft.	1851	$30,000	$16.19
M. Mott & Co. at head of						
Virginia Bar	59	16	10	296	8,000	27.00
Centennial P. M. -						
above Lum Grey Mott & Co.						
	685	40	40	40,000	97,000	2.42
Manzanita Bar, Mott Co.						
	1600	200	25	296,296	300,000	1.01
Spengler P.M. - at the mouth of Humbug Crk.						
from 7 acres				203,280	234,858	1.10
MINES BELOW BEAVER CREEK						
Yankee Dam, below Horse Creek,						
Vatinell Co.	100	60	4	888	13,000	14.62
Pierson Co. below O.B.						
	150	20	3	836	7,300	8.72
Vatinell Co.	150	60	6	1,666	8,000	4.80
M.Mott Co.	150	20	6	10,666	3,300	4.95
Poverty Point Drift Mine						
across from Oak Bar						
	1,500	30	6	10,000	23,000	2.36
Maplesden Wingdam, below						
McKinney Creek	150	30	30	5,000	30,000	6.00
China Sam Co., above McKinney						
Creek, joins P.G.P.M- taken						
out in one wingdam						
	250	50	8	3,703	25,000	6.75

	Size of Ground Worked		No. Cu.	Taken	Value per	Average
	Length	Width	Depth	yds	Out	YD.
Oak Bar P.M. - Kleaver & Portuguese Co.						
	600	200	10	44,444	60,000	1.12
Buckeye Bar P.M. - below P.GP.M.						
	200	50	5	1,851	25,000	13.50
Kols, Wingdam, Oak Bar						
	100	30	6	666	600	.90
Kols Wingdam below Oak Bar						
	60	30	6	400	1,100	2.75
				621,843	$866,158.00	

From 621,843 cu. yds. was taken $866,158 or an average of one dollar and forty-three cents ($1.43).

Wm. Kleaver & Co. took out with 11 men and use of derrick, by hand shoveling, in one day, 48 ounces, or $804.00

Portuguese Co. took out with 11 men and use of derrick, in 3 days, by hand, shoveling, at Oak Bar, $3,000 or 1,000 per day.

China Sam Co. took out in one tube of gravel or one cu. yd., (just below Pine Grove P.M.) 8 ounces of gold, valued at $134.00.

Wm. McConnel claim at mouth of Humbug Creek took out one season $34,000: another season, $28,000; and still another $22,000. This work was done by pick and shovel and use of derrick and all taken from about one acre of ground.

TRINITY COUNTY

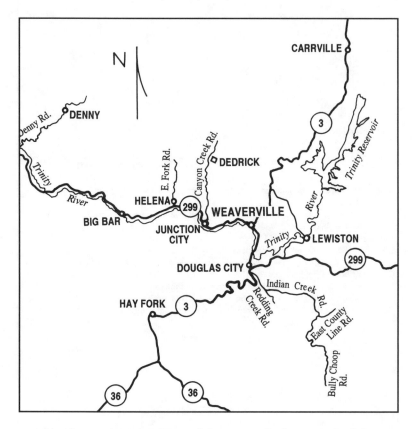

You're going to love this area. It has everything a prospector could want. Lots of water, many gold sites, lots of history, and places for supplies. The locals will tell you, "Life is good here, it moves along at a less hectic pace." There are no freeways, stop lights, or traffic jams, and friendly locals will even stop to let you cross the street. Bring some warm clothes because even in summer the evenings can get chilly. There are some campgrounds to make base camp here. We stay at the Douglas City campground most of the time because it is easy to work many of the areas both here and in Shasta County. There are no showers there but you can jump into the river to wash off, but let me warn you, the river is cold most of the time. Douglas City is also the area where the first gold was discovered in Trinity County. Major Pierson Reading discovered the placer deposits here in 1848. He took out $80,000 in gold in only six weeks. When word got out of the rich diggings the rush to this region began. There is a marker right by the campground marking the discovery. Estimated gold production for the county is set at over $75,000,000. There are lots of large tailing piles for the nugget shooter to work here in the various areas, and some large nuggets have been found here. One of the largest was worth $1,800 at the old price of gold, found on Digger Creek, so bring along your metal detector as well as your pan. During the Depression, quite a few people made enough to live on working the old deposits in the county and experts agree that none of the areas has been worked out.

BIG BAR

This area is now included in the Trinity River district. It is a small placer mining region. Nothing remains of the original camp site but there are lots of tailing piles here to testify to its early importance. The camp was located at the place where Big Bar Creek and the Trinity River join. The gold is found in the recent stream gravels and in the bench deposits. Big Bar and Weaverville were the first two places in the county to get a post office. Big Bar was located across the river from Big Flat. To reach this area, go west out of Junction City on Highway 299.

BULLY CHOOP

This a small lode mining district in the southern portion of the county. The mines were worked beginning in the 1880s and were active up into the early 1900s. The gold-quartz veins are not large but extend a good distance in some cases. Take Reading Creek Road off of Highway 3 south of Douglas City to the forks, take the left fork which is Indian Creek Road. It is about 15 miles south of Weaverville.

CARRVILLE

The Carrville area is also now included in the Trinity River district. Named for the Carr family who were active miners in the region, it is a placer and lode gold mining area. Gold was first discovered here in 1852, but most of the production came from the latter part of the 1800s and lasted well into the 1900s. The placer deposits are in the recent stream gravels and the bank deposits. The veins are gold-quartz. Take Highway 3 north out of Weaverville to reach Carrville.

COFFEE CREEK

Another Coffee Creek, the name is not quite as common as Dry Creek but it comes close. This Coffee Creek is in northeast Trinity County near Carrville. Mainly a placer mining area there have been a few gold-quartz veins worked here. The Holland mine here had over two miles of the east fork of Coffee Creek claimed up and operated for 50 years. Numerous gold nuggets valued at over $200 each are found in the gravels every year here. The placer deposits were discovered in the 1850s and work has been done here off and on ever since. Take Highway 3 north out of Weaverville to Coffee Creek Road and turn left. This will take you into the area.

DEDRICK-CANYON CREEK

Canyon Creek is a popular area for prospectors today. It is a placer mining district that was first worked in the early part of the Gold Rush. Work of some sort has gone on here ever since then. The gold is in the present stream gravels and the bench deposits. The bench deposits have been hydraulic mined and have produced very well. Most all the gulches feeding into the creek have contained gold. Junction City, where Canyon Creek joins the Trinity River, was called the liveliest town in the county in 1895 by the Trinity Journal newspaper. The paper also said that mining was flourishing along the creek at that time. Take Canyon Creek Road north off of Highway 299. It follows the creek.

Dedrick is a small lode mining district north of Junction City. Even though the town wasn't established until 1891, nothing remains of the old camp today. The town was named for a prospector, named D.C. Dedrick, who discovered the Chloride Mine vein in the 1880s. The gold-quartz veins are not large but have had some rich pockets. They are sometimes found in hornblende. Take Canyon Creek Road north from Highway 299 at Junction City to reach the Dedrick area. It is in the national forest a little before you reach Ripstein Campground.

HAYFORK

This district is now included in the Trinity River District. I thought I would list it here because there have been reports of some nice little nuggets being found here in recent years. The placer gold is found in Hayfork Creek and other creeks in the area around the town of Hayfork. Some narrow gold-quartz veins have been found in the mountains south of Hayfork. The veins are narrow, but rich in spots, and in slate. Take Highway 3 south off of Highway 299 at Douglas City to reach Hayfork.

HELENA-EAST FORK

An interesting note to this area is a recent discovery while building the bridge here of the remains of an ancient Indian campsite where Helena is. The Indian campsite dates back nearly 4,000 years. The first recorded gold found here was in the early part of the Gold Rush in the stream gravels. There has been some lode mining done here as well. The bench deposits on the east fork of the river were pretty productive and worth checking out again. Helena is worth visiting for the old Gold Rush buildings remaining. Bagdad was a campsite nearby. We have detected there and found a few old coins, but darn it, no nuggets! The gold-quartz veins have contained some rich pockets. Take Highway 299 west out of Weaverville about 20 miles to reach Helena. Take the East Fork Road north off of Highway 299 to reach this area.

NEW RIVER - DENNY

The placer deposits on the New River were first worked in 1849 and produced quite a bit of gold for several years. There were two rushes to the New River, the first during the Gold Rush. There were 300 miners panning, sluicing, and working with rockers all over the river. As the easily worked gravels were depleted, the miners moved on and by 1875 only 15 miners were working claims there. Soon after that in the early 1880s, new rich deposits were found and a new rush began to the area. Three towns sprang up and it was busy place. By 1920 all the towns were abandoned again. Maybe it is ready for a new rush. Hoboken was an important camp site in the early days and was located on a flat about seven miles upstream from the mouth of the New River. Denny was originally called New River City and was established in the 1880s when rich lode deposits were discovered there. The placer deposits are in the recent stream gravels and the bank deposits. The lode gold veins are gold-quartz and found in slate and greenstone. Take the Denny Road north out of Hawkin's Bar off of Highway 299 to reach this area.

TRINITY RIVER

Like the Klamath River, a lot of the old gold districts are now included in one large district and called the Trinity River District. The Trinity River has produced large amounts of placer gold for prospectors over the years. There are also some lode mining areas included in this district. The old districts now included in this district are the Big Bar, Burnt Ranch, Carrville, Dodge, Douglas City, Eastman Gulch, Hayfork, Junction City, Lewiston, Minersville, Salyer, Stuart Fork, and Trinity Center. Lewiston, for example, is the third largest community in Trinity County and began as an early mining camp in the 1850s. The first bridge in Trinity County was built here by the miners in 1851. It got washed away, as did several built after it. Lewiston was mainly a placer mining area. Minersville is now under Trinity Lake. The river starts around the old camp of Dodge and flows for almost 60 miles across gold bearing rocks that create the placer deposits. Over 1 million ounces of gold have come out of the river since the Gold Rush. The placer deposits are found in the recent stream gravels as well as the bench deposits. Most all of the creeks, such as Weaver Creek, Indian Creek, Reading Creek, Coffee Creek, and others that feed the river, have been rich in places. The richest bench gravels are at Hocker Flat, Benjamin Flat, Chapman Ranch, and Coopers Bars. Most all the many bars along the river were very rich. The veins are gold-quartz and are found in slate and greenstone in many areas. Highway 299 follows the river for quite a few miles and many of the mining sites are along this route.

The Weaverville Museum

WEAVERVILLE

The area of Weaverville charmed people in the Gold Rush and still charms people today. James Hilton who coined the phrase "Shangri La" in his book, *Lost Horizon*, said that Weaverville was the closest to "Shangri La" as anyplace he had found in traveling all over the world. After Major Reading found gold near here in 1848, miners rushed to the area in droves to work the gold rich streams and soon a camp was established. The district was a major source of gold production in the Klamath Mountains for years. The first residents lived in tents but soon cabins were being built and stores set up. By 1854, the town had twenty-two stores, two banks, two drugstores, six saloons, six hotels, four restaurants, and other businesses, and a population of 1,000, which didn't count the many Chinese working here then. The Chinese Tong War of 1854 took place here when about 600 Chinese took part in a battle on a flat near Five Cent Creek. There was a lot of noise but not a lot of injuries. Weaverville is the county seat and has been since the county was established. The La Grange Mine a few miles west of the town is one of the largest hydraulic mines in the state. The gravels containing the gold were very rich and as thick as 400 feet. There are a few gold-quartz veins in diorite and Birds-eye porphyry dikes found here. Experts say that there are still some original gravels unworked left here. Look for the blue-quartz gravels as they are the richest. Weaverville is on Highway 299 west of Redding. You can't miss it.

ROCK AND GEM SITES

You can find serpentine, rhonite, feldspar, and native copper ore along Coffee Creek. Take the Coffee Creek Road off of Highway 3 north of Trinity Center. The collecting area is on both sides of the creek where the public land begins and goes up the creek sides quite a ways. Jasper and agate are found along the Mad River banks and the surrounding areas. The area near the small town of Ruth is one of the better collecting areas.

TREASURE TALES

A Wells Fargo packtrain carrying $80,000 in gold from the mines in Yreka was held up near the edge of Trinity Mountain. They took the mules carrying the gold and fled. The Wells Fargo men got to Shasta and told the story of the robbery to the town people. A posse was formed at once and set out after the outlaws. When the posse got to Clear Creek they found the saddlebags that the pack mules had been carrying the gold in–empty, of course. The bandits had been led by Rattlesnake Dick, a well-known bandit of the day. The gang got trapped on the side of Trinity Mountain and one of the bandits went into the trees and buried half the loot. They didn't want to be slowed down by the heavy gold and figured they would come back and get the rest of the gold when things cooled down. The posse spotted them riding away and a running gun fight took place and the bandit who had hidden the gold was killed. The area where the gold is thought to be buried is 12 miles south of Clear Creek.

In the area around the lower end of Haman Ridge in southwestern Trinity County, a soldier's gambling winnings and six months' pay is said to be buried. According to the story, the soldiers were on patrol and had just gotten six months' back pay. One night they got into a poker game and one of the soldiers won almost everyone's money. He didn't want to carry all the money with him so he buried it under a tree for safekeeping. He picked a tree that had been struck by lightning so he could find it again easily. The next day the man was killed in a battle with Indians. No one could find the tree again and the money is still there. It would be worth a great deal because it was in gold and silver coins mainly.

HISTORICAL SITES

The Weaverville Joss House State Historical Park is located right in town and is an interesting place to visit. The present Joss House was built in 1874 and is in great condition.

The La Grange hydraulic mine is also listed as a state historical landmark. It is about four miles west of Weaverville on Highway 299.

La Grange Hydralic Mine, Weaverville District. This northward view of the mine, in Trinity County, was taken about 1914. La Grange was one of the largest hydralic mines in the state.
(Reprinted, by permission, from California Division of Mines and Geology, *Gold Districts of California*, 145)

OTHER AREAS

There are several other counties in northern California that have produced significant amounts of gold in the past. Some of these counties have only one or two gold bearing areas so we are combining them in this chapter. Since they have produced gold in the past they are worth investigating by the prospector. You never know when some lucky miner might start another Gold Rush.

MENDOCINO COUNTY

Mendocino is one of the original 27 counties in California. Ukiah has always been the county seat. It has one gold district.

RED MOUNTAIN

Red Mountain is south and east of Ukiah almost on the border of Mendocino County and Lake Country. Placer gold has been found in the streams in the area along the slopes of the mountains. There are some quartz veins containing gold and copper found here as well. Go south on Highway 101 a few miles. Red Mountain is on the east side of the highway.

MODOC COUNTY

Modoc County was formed in 1874 from a portion of Siskiyou County. Alturas has always been the county seat. There are two gold districts in the county.

HIGH GRADE

This is a small lode mining district in the Warner Mountains in northern Modoc County. It was first called the Hoag District after the prospector who made the first discovery. The veins were not discovered till 1905. There was quite a bit of activity here shortly after that and prospecting continued until the late 1930s. Prospectors still worked the area looking to make another good strike. The gold-quartz veins found in rhyolite are narrow and do not go to any great length. The Warner Mountains are near the Oregon border about 10 miles north of Fort Bidwell. Take the Highgrade Road east off of Highway 395 right before the state line.

WINTERS

Another small lode mining district it is located in southwestern Modoc County. The veins were discovered in the late 1800s. The main mine in the area was the Lost Cabin which was located in 1904. Prospecting has occurred here off and on since then. The gold-quartz veins are not very large and do not go to any great depth. Take Highway 299 north out of Adin about 15 miles. The mines are located on your right hand or eastern side of the highway.

MONTEREY COUNTY

Another of the original 27 California counties, Monterey County, is mostly associated with early California history, but some gold has been mined here.

JOLAN

This is a small placer mining district in the southern part of Monterey County. Most of the activity took place around the present Mission San Antonio de Padua which was built in 1810. Jolan was a way station on the stage road between Los Angeles and San Francisco. The stream deposits were worked as early as 1850. In the late 1870s the area was worked by Chinese miners and several thousand dollars worth of gold was recovered. There were a lot of nice-sized nuggets found here. The gold is fairly coarse so there must be some veins nearby. Try working in Mission and Ruby Canyons or any of the gulches draining the Santa Lucia Mountains. Take Highway 101 north out of Paso Robles to Road G18. This will take you to Jolan.

LOS BURROS

This a fairly active district in the Santa Lucia Mountains. The placer deposits were worked early in the 1850s and continue up to today. The first lode deposits were discovered in 1887 and created a great deal of excitement for the next few years. Willow Creek has produced the most gold, but gold has also been found in Salmon Creek, Plaskitt Creek, and Alder Creek. It is found in Willow Creek in its main body and its forks. The lode deposits are gold-quartz veins found mainly in sandstone. At one time there were claims everywhere in this area but a lot have lapsed. The area can be reach by going south on Highway 1 out of Monterey for about 80 miles. The deposits are in the mountains about three to four miles to the east from the Cape San Martin area.

NAPA COUNTY

Napa County is noted more for its wines than its gold. Napa was the name of the Indian tribe that first occupied the area.

CALISTOGA

Named by Sam Brannan who helped start the Gold Rush to the Mother Lode country, Calistoga is a small gold-silver lode mining district. Brannan established a resort on the hot springs there in 1859 after making a fortune selling equipment to the miners. The veins were not worked until the 1870s and most of the production has come from two mines, the Silverado, and the Palisade. Of the two, the Palisade was the most productive. Production for the district is over $500,000. The quartz veins are good-sized and contain some rich pockets. The veins are found on the east side of Mt. St. Helena. Take Highway 12 off of Highway 80 out of Oakland to Highway 29. It is east of Sugar Loaf Ridge State Park.

SACRAMENTO COUNTY

For only having a couple of gold districts, Sacramento County has produced an awful lot of gold. The history of gold in California really began here at Sutter's Fort when John Sutter sent James Marshall to build him a sawmill on the American River and Marshall found that first piece of gold that started it all. Sacramento County is in the top ten in gold production by counties in the state with recorded production of over $135,000,000. Mormon Bar in the northeast portion of the county was the site of the second important gold discovery in California. Two Mormons stopped there on their way to Sutter's Fort and found gold in 1848, soon after the discovery at Sutter's Mill. Sam Brannan jumped their claim and soon started to accumulate the wealth that would make him one of the richest men in early California history. The area is now under Folsom Lake.

FOLSOM

The first miners here were a group of black men and the camp was called Negro Bar. The men first worked the placer deposits in 1849, and by 1851 the camp had a population of 700. Most of the early production came from working the placers by hand methods such as panning and sluicing. Later in the 1890s, bucket line dredging began and continued until 1962 when the last dredge shut down.

Estimated production is set at $125,000,000. Other nearby areas such as Willow Springs and Alder Creek were also very productive in the early days. The dredging fields are 10 miles long and seven miles wide. Most of this area has been built over now. The placer deposits are in the stream gravels. A few small gold-quartz veins are found in greenstone east of Folsom. Take Highway 50 east out of Sacramento to reach this area.

Natomas Company Dredge No. 2, Folsom District.
This 1921 view of the dredge, in Sacramento County,
shows the double stackers and sand wheel.
(Courtesy of C.A. Waring)

MICHIGAN BAR

Michigan Bar is located on the Cosumnes River in the eastern part of Sacramento County. The original townsite was washed away by the hydraulic mining done later in the area. Mining camps nearby were Cook's Bar, Sebastopol, Katesville, and Live Oak. The Sloughhouse area is also included in this district. The gold is found in the recent stream gravels and the bench deposits. Take Highway 16 east out of Sacramento to Michigan Bar Road and go north. This will take you right to the area. The Cosumnes River crosses the road.

SAN FRANCISCO COUNTY

There is only one gold district in San Francisco County and that is San Francisco Beach. You will find fine gold in the black sand on San Francisco Beach. Your best bet is to try your luck after a rainstorm. The best area is south along the beach from the Fleishhacker Zoo. There have been reports of gold-quartz veins being found here but there is no reported production from them.

SONOMA COUNTY

The only reported gold production from Sonoma County came in the late 1800s from the Silver Queen Mine. There have been small amounts of placer gold found here in the past. Take Fort Ross Road east out of Fort Ross to the Cazedero Road. This is the general area to search.

TEHAMA COUNTY

Tehama County was created from Butte County, Colusa County, and Shasta County.

Red Bluff has been the county seat since 1857. There are two gold districts in Tehama County.

JELLY FERRY

This is a small placer mining district on the Sacramento River north of Red Bluff. The gravels were worked early in the Gold Rush and later by the Chinese miners. Some large scale dredging was tried here but it was not successful. The gold is found in recent stream gravels and in the terrace deposits. Go north on Highway 5 out of Red Bluff to Jelly Ferry Road. This road will take you into the area.

POLK SPRINGS

Another small placer mining area is located in eastern Tehama County. There was some hydraulic mining done here in the early days with fair results. Nothing has been done here for several years. Deer Creek has produced gold from the stream gravels and the bank deposits. Take Highway 36 east out of Red Bluff to Plum Creek Road and go right on this road to Ponderosa Way Road. Go right on this road and it will take you to the area.

YOLO COUNTY

This is another of the first counties established in the State. The county seat is Woodland. There is only one gold district in Yolo County. The Putah Creek district is located in southeastern Yolo County. Most of the mining was done in the 1800s but there was some activity here in the 1930s, as there was in most areas during the Depression. There was a campsite at the point that the creek enters the valley, but nothing remains of it today. There was also gold found in other areas in the region like Cache Creek. A few gold-quartz veins have been reported in the mountains nearby. Take Highway 505 north off of Highway 80 between Oakland and Sacramento to Highway 128. Go past Winters and the road will run along side Putah Creek all the way to the Montecell Dam.

4. How to Find Gold

Equipment

The Gold Pan

Regardless of whether you are a new prospector or a pro, the gold pan is still the most indispensable companion you can have. It is one of the first tools used in locating gold and is one of the last used, even in commercial mining, to check the value of ore being processed. The gold pan is used wherever gold occurs in approximately 75% of all the countries in the world.

As far as we know, the BATEA, a conical-shaped gold pan, was the first pan to be used. It was developed by the Mayan Indian civilization. The Batea is some fifteen or sixteen inches in diameter, and six to eight inches deep. The early ones were carved from wood. They were used to pan gold, diamonds, emeralds, and rubies. Anything heavier than common sand and gravel could be panned with this device. The Batea is an unwieldy and very heavy device requiring a great deal of experience before it can be used efficiently. For this reason it never gained much popularity outside of South and Central America.

In the early days of prospecting in this country, the pan was commonly called the "gold dish." Many prospectors carved their own from a large block of wood. It didn't take many sophisticated tools to make a wooden pan—just a jackknife to do the rough carving, which could then be "sanded" smooth with gravel from a streambed.

Cowhorns were also used to make gold pans. Carefully slit lengthwise, and then steamed until it was soft enough to be worked, the horn was opened out and shaped into a shallow dish suitable for panning. In the old days the "gold dish" was the only means available to the small miner and prospector for the separation of gold.

Until just recently, the most popular pan to evolve was the steel pan. It is manufactured by a metal "spinning" process. This was a far cry from the crude hand-forged pans that the local blacksmith used to make.

Probably the most efficient pan for the novice today is one molded from tough, space age plastic. It is far superior to the steel pan for several reasons. First, it is rust and corrosive proof. Secondly, it can be textured with a fine "tooth" surface to hold the gold better. Third, it is about one-quarter the weight of a steel pan, and fourth, the color can be made a permanent black so that even the tiniest flakes of gold can easily be seen.

Any of the above reasons are sufficient to endorse the plastic pan. But there is still another advantage. Being made by an injection mold process, riffles can be easily formed into a plastic pan. These riffles trap the gold much as the riffles in a sluice box, thus speeding up the panning process considerably. Old timers often refer to these as "cheater riffles" because they allow the novice to pan with nearly the same degree of efficiency it took the old timers years to develop.

The common sizes of pans today are the six to ten inch pan, used primarily for sampling, the twelve to fourteen inch pan often used by novices, and the sixteen to eighteen inch pan used by the more experienced panners. The larger pan load requires much greater stamina and technique.

An accomplished professional panner can only process about one cubic yard of material in a 10-hour day. But with the development of the hand sluice, the dredge, and the rocker, even the novice today can process about 3/4 of a cubic yard per hour.

Even with the more sophisticated equipment, the pan is still necessary to clean up the sluice box. With the pan the concentrate is worked to a point where the large gold can be removed, leaving only a black or very heavy sand. This sand should always be kept for later separation by jigging or some kind of a tabling process capable of salvaging gold sized at 100 mesh or above which would be very difficult to recover by panning. Save those black sand concentrates! They can be worth anywhere from one to ten dollars a pound, making it a very valuable commodity, indeed.

Recreational "mining" is one of the fastest growing hobbies in the U.S.A. today, and here the gold pan is the prime tool! There are many large resorts throughout the world where the activities center mainly around gold panning. There are probably somewhere in the neighborhood of 3,000,000 gold pans sold annually in this country alone.

Trying your luck at panning could lead to one of the most fascinating, enjoyable hobbies you have ever known. The gamble of taking a pan full of material and finding precious metal in any quantity, whether only a flake or laden with nuggets, is a sensation that is unexplainable.

The Plastic Gold Pan. Note the built-in "cheater riffles" on the side of the pan for easier panning.
(Courtesy of Keene Engineering)

Panning Instructions

Before you actually start to process your first pan full of material, look around for the best location for panning. Select a spot where the water is a minimum of six inches deep and flowing just fast enough to keep the muddy water from impairing your vision of your pan and a place where you can sit down comfortably.

STEP A – WASHING OFF LARGER ROCKS AND MOSS

1. Fill pan 3/4 full of gravel, then submerge it deep enough so it is just under the surface of the water. Give the pan several vigorous shakes back and forth and from side to side, but not too vigorous as to wash material out of the pan.

Step A - #1. Submerge and shake the pan.

2. Change from the shaking motion to a gentle circular movement, so the material starts revolving in a circle. This process will cause most of the dirt and clay to dissolve and wash out of the pan. If roots and moss surface, work them over your pan with your fingers to dissolve any lumps. Pick out the larger rocks after making sure that they are washed clean.

Step A - #2. Picking out the large rocks.

Repeat processes 1 and 2 of step A to get the smaller rock to the surface and to cause the heavier concentrates to settle.

STEP B – WASHING OFF LIGHTER SAND AND GRAVEL

1. Hold the pan just under the water and tilt it slightly away from you. Begin to swirl the water from side to side, with a slight forward tossing motion. Take care, but swirl with sufficient force to move the surface and lighter gravel out over the edge of the pan.

Step B - #1. Tilting the pan and swirling the water.

2.   Leveling the pan from time to time and shaking it back and forth will cause the light material to come to the surface and the gold to settle to the bottom.

Step B - # 2. Leveling the pan.

Repeat process 1 and 2 of step B until there are only about two cups of heavier material left in your pan. This material is usually called "black sand," or "concentrate."

STEP C – WASHING OFF BLACK
SAND AND CONCENTRATES

At this point it is better for the beginner to raise the pan completely out of the water, leaving about an inch of water in it. Tilt the pan slightly towards you and swirl the water slowly in a circular motion to check the pan for nuggets and pieces that are easily picked out by hand.

Then submerge the pan again in water and repeat process 1 and 2 of step B for final concentration. This is the most critical part of panning. Make sure this final process is accomplished with as much diligence as possible so you do not to wash out the gold.

If you have a plastic pan, the use of a magnet can be employed to quickly aid in the separation of gold from the black magnetic sand concentrate.

Apply the magnet to the bottom side of the pan and move it in a small circular motion with the pan slightly tilted. This will swiftly isolate the gold from the black sand.

PANNING HINTS

When using a steel pan, make sure to remove all the oil from the pan before you use it. The most common way is to "burn" it over the coals of a campfire. The pan is heated to a dull red glow, then dunked in water. This not only removes the oil but also gives the pan a dark blue hue, which makes the gold easier to see. If any oil is left in the pan, it will cause the fine gold to float, making separation impossible.

Another secret to speed up the final steps is to keep a small squeeze bottle of detergent close at hand. A couple of drops in the pan during the last separation will break the surface tension of the water and speed up the operation considerably.

In conclusion, don't let anyone tell you that this country's rivers and streams no longer contain gold. Every year winter storms bring more to the surface, continually renewing nature's supply. It's all there for the taking, and the gold pan is still the best way to find it!

An item that is considered a necessary part of a panners equipment is a panning sieve. The sieve sets over the pan and can screen or classify the larger cobbles, making the panning process much easier.

The gold pan sieves are most popular with the medium- size pan and are available in most prospecting stores that sell gold recovery equipment.

Panning for gold.

The Sluice Box

There are many methods of prospecting for gold. Many people dredge or dry-wash for it, while other prospectors use electronic metal detection equipment in their search for the precious yellow metal. One of the most practical methods of gold prospecting and recovery involves the use of a piece of equipment that has been in use for over a hundred years. One of the very best gold gathering devices on the market today is the Hand Sluice.

Sluice boxes were once built at the location of the mining site from the material that was on hand, such as heavy wood planks and logs. Often the river current was diverted through them so that gold-bearing gravels could be processed far quicker than using the laborious "hand panning" method.

The old sluice boxes were lined with raised obstructions that were placed in a vertical position to the flow of the current. (These obstructions were later referred to as riffles.) When the gold-laden gravels were dumped into the upper end of the sluice, the flow of water carried the material down the length of the box. The lighter gravels (tailings) would be carried in suspension down the entire length of the sluice and then discharged. The heavier material (such as gold, platinum metals and black sands), would quickly drop to the bottom of the box, where they became entrapped by the riffles. Once the riffles collected a large quantity of concentrated black sand, a "cleanup" was implemented. The flow of water through the sluice would be diminished by a type of water gate. Then the riffles would be removed, allowing access to the heavier materials which had collected during the "run." This remaining material or concentrate often contained all the values amounting to many tons of gravel which had to be tediously panned.

The sluice boxes in the days of the 49'ers were very similar to the ones of today. The primary difference is the

Power Sluice Concentrator. (Courtesy of Keene Engineering)

Hand Sluice Box with Superheavy Duty Riffle Latches.
(Courtesy Keene Engineering)

construction and materials. Sluice boxes were built of heavy wood planks, because lumber was cheap and easily obtainable. Today's sluice boxes are constructed of lightweight aluminum and steel.

Any miner will tell you that portability is the key to success. Most of the gold deposits that are accessible have long since been depleted of their gold. Today you will have to hike in to find any virgin areas.

During the Gold Rush, sluices were first used to work the extremely rich bench deposits, "terrace gravels," which lined the banks of many Mother Lode rivers. As time passed it became clear that sluice boxes could be used for working other types of gold-bearing material, to include ancient river channel deposits located hundreds of feet above the existing streambeds. Modern prospectors use sluice boxes to work literally any type of gold-bearing gravel which cannot be worked with a suction dredge. Sluice boxes have been successfully used to process gold bearing gravels located in dry deserts with trucked-in water and recirculation systems.

In many cases, today's prospectors use their sluice boxes to work areas located adjacent to flowing streams. Frequently, people who own suction dredges will carry in a lightweight sluice box to sample gravel bars they may wish to dredge later on. If it turns out a gravel bar is not as rich as originally believed, all the labor of carrying in a large dredge is avoided.

For the benefit of those who are not familiar with the proper use of a sluice box, I will explain the basic principles involved. As you will learn shortly, they are not the least bit complicated. Anyone can become a qualified "sluice tender" after just a few hours time spent in the field!

111

Sluicing Instructions

STEP 1 – GETTING SET UP

After you have located a promising deposit of gold-bearing gravel, walk along the stream bank and look for a place where you can set up your sluice box. You should search for a spot where the current is moving quite swiftly. Once you find such a place, set your sluice box directly in the current so that the box is filled with water almost to the top. You can often compensate by placing the sluice box so that the upper "input" end is slightly higher than the lower "discharge" end. If the sluice box is somewhat unstable in the current, position a few rocks around the outside of the trough to brace it.

Sometimes you will not even need the "rock brace," as the first bucket of gravel dumped into the sluice box will provide just enough heavy iron sand to weigh it down.

STEP 2 – FEEDING THE SLUICE

Feed your gold-bearing gravel into the upper portion of the sluice box in carefully regulated amounts. Do not, under any circumstances, dump a very large amount of gravel into the sluice box all at once! The gravel must be fed at a pace that will not overload the riffles. How can you tell when the riffles are overloading? It is simple. If you cannot see the uppermost "crest" of each riffle bar at all times, you are feeding the gravel too fast. Back off a bit. The penalty for overloading your riffles is something not very pleasant: lost gold! Each time a new load of gravel is dumped into a sluice box with overloaded riffles, any gold in that gravel will wash right over the material that is clogging your riffles and out the discharge end of the box. Remember, don't overload your riffles!

STEP 3 – TENDING THE SLUICE

After dumping each load of gravel into the sluice box, check the riffle section for large waste rocks that may be hanging up. Flick these rocks out of the riffles with your fingers. When large rocks are allowed to rest in the riffle section they will cause the current to wash out all the concentrates from the immediate area of the rock. If a rock is lodged in the uppermost portion of the trough, the washed out concentrates will merely settle in the next few riffles down. But if the wash-out occurs at the lower end of the trough, the concentrate may flow out of the sluice box altogether. As one can see, it pays to keep an eye on those waste rocks! And one more thing, don't forget to shovel away the tailings which will periodically build up at the discharge end of the sluice box. If you don't the tailings will back up into the lower end of the sluice trough, burying some of your riffles.

STEP 4 – PERFORMING THE CLEANUP

When your riffles have accumulated black iron sand in amounts extending more than halfway downward to the next lower bar, it is time to perform a cleanup. Carefully lift the sluice box from the current, keeping it as level as possible. Now carry it over to the stream bank (watch your footing on those slippery rocks!) and set it down. Remove the sluice's riffle section and set it aside, exercising care not to shake off any gravel adhering to it. Roll up the matting which lines the bottom of the sluice box trough and thoroughly rinse off all the concentrate. This should be done with the matting safely contained in a deep bucket. Doing it this way will ensure recovery of all gold that ordinarily would be lost when attempting to rinse out the matting in a gold pan! Next, examine the empty sluice box trough. Is there any fine silt clinging to the bottom? If there is, rinse all of it into your concentrate bucket. Gold has a tendency to work its way beneath the matting which lies between the riffle bars and the bottom of the trough, and you would be surprised at the amount of "color" that can accumulate there.

Finally, pick up the riffle section itself and rinse any adhering gravel into the concentrate bucket. The sluice box cannot be considered "cleaned" until each and every part has been thoroughly rinsed.

STEP 5 – GETTING THE GOLD OUT

And now for the final step. This is the one you will certainly enjoy the most. The act of panning out your concentrates to get the gold. I hope your run was a profitable one!

SUMMING UP

By the time you get to Step Five, you will have processed several hundred pounds of gravel, far more than the average person could ever hope to hand-pan during a daily outing. Using a sluice box you can work as much gravel in an hour as you can pan in a day. All you need is a sturdy shovel, a couple of good buckets to carry gravel to the creek, a mining partner to feed the sluice box while you dig gravel, and a solid desire to get that gold.

Happy sluicing!

Dredging

In the beginning of the Gold Rush, the miners were limited because they could only work the areas that were accessible to hand tools along the banks of the streams and rivers. Their equipment was limited to gold pans, sluice boxes and rockers. As time progressed and as they became more experienced, they realized that the deeper gravels in the riverbeds were often richer than the surface gravel along the banks.

In the early 1900s, several crudely built steam powered dredges were active on some of the northern rivers of California. The divers worked futilely on the bottom of the rivers with heavy diving helmets and cumbersome diving suits.

Although history reveals that dredging has been in existence throughout the world for many years, it is just recently that it has reached such a high degree of popularity due to advanced technology in dredging equipment. Dredges of today are lighter, more portable and more efficient than ever.

A backpack dredge of today can weigh as little as forty pounds and cost only a little more than seven hundred dollars. It can process as much gravel as a three hundred pound unit could some twenty years ago. One of the most exciting features of this type of dredge is that it allows the prospector to penetrate areas that were otherwise impossible to reach with heavier and more cumbersome equipment.

They are also far more efficient than the machines of old. It is not uncommon to see a dredge profitably working the tailings of some of the old mines and tailing dumps.

There are two basic types of dredges on the market today. They are the surface dredge and the underwater submersible dredge. The surface dredge is the most popular and the most efficient gold saver.

The Underwater Dredge

The underwater dredge is the less popular, mainly because it lacks somewhat in its ability to recover gold as fine as the surface type. It is designed mainly for compactness and portability, but is limited also in its application as it is cumbersome to handle underwater. The submersible dredge must be held perfectly level while in operation and cannot reach around corners and hard to get at places.

Tony Simpson of Tee Dee Co. working his own Dredge.

It also is not practical to use in very shallow water, as it must be completely submerged to operate properly. It is best described as a flared metal or plastic tube with a forty five to sixty degree bend on the end where water is inducted at high pressure creating a vacuum at the end of the bend. A high pressure water pump is located normally on a float that sits at the surface of the water and is pumped down to the dredge via a high pressure hose. At the end of the flared tube a riffle tray is attached containing a series of gold traps. As the gold bearing gravel is sucked into the dredge the heavier particles, including gold, become entrapped in the riffle tray. The lighter non-gold-bearing particles flow back into the river. The submersible dredge of today is mainly used for sampling; and when a good streak is found, the surface dredge is employed to do a more efficient job.

Pat Keene with Dredge.

The Surface Dredge

The surface dredge rests on the surface of the water. The material is pumped to the surface by way of a suction hose into a larger and more efficient sluice box. The sluice box can either rest on the bank, that is common on some of the smaller units, or floated on the water with inflatable tubes or commercially-made Marlex floats. The Marlex floats are preferred in most cases as they are more stable, rugged and are designed specifically for dredging. The inner tube has one important feature, it can be deflated and more easily packed, the bad news is they also can easily become punctured. Another advantage of the surface dredge is that it can easily be operated without the use of diving equipment, unlike the submersible type. An operator can work from the surface easily with only boots or waders to insulate him from potentially cold water.

Of the many types of surface dredges available today, the triple and double sluices are the most popular, because they have a greater capacity to recover a much finer grade of gold and black sand concentrates. The triple sluices are found in the larger style dredges from four inches and up. Normally, the lesser size dredges from three inches and smaller are equipped with double sluices. Black sand concentrates are sought after today, because they often contain particles of micron gold. Frequently these concentrates may be worth anywhere from one dollar to twenty dollars per pound. This is especially important in the larger dredges where large quantities of gravel are processed. Often this may not be an important factor with small dredges due to their limited capacity of processing gravel.

What is a TRIPLE OR DOUBLE SLUICE DREDGE? I thought you would never ask! The basic difference between a single and a double or triple sluice is that the single sluice processes all the material through the single sluice box without minimal classification. The double and triple classify and size the material before it enters the recovery section of the sluice box. This is a most important feature because often, the high velocity that is required to move the larger rocks and gravel through the sluice can carry some of the fine gold back into the river. In order to recover fine gold in a sluice box it is important to run the smaller gravel as slow as possible without causing a build-up of excess waste material. If properly designed, a sluice box will self-clean and operate for hours on end without intermittent cleaning.

The Dry Washer

Dry washers are most popular in areas where water is not available, such as dry washes and desert areas.

A dry washer utilizes air, vibration and static electricity to very effectively separate gold from the waste gravel.

The use of vibration to move material through a sluice box is similar to the same movement created by water velocity. This method of dry recovery can be extremely effective when the proper balance of air separation and vibration is employed.

The concept of air separation is also vital to proper dry recovery, as vibration alone cannot create proper separation. If air is induced properly it can create a static charge that will create a magnetic field that will attract only heavy metals such as gold. This static charge is created when it is forced through a special fibrous material that lines the recovery trough of the dry washer.

You can purchase one that is manufactured or attempt to build your own. I have owned a Keene Electrostatic Concentrator for several years. For my money, it is the best portable dry washer made. It works on a greater principal than a regular dry washer. The concentrator is driven by a high-speed blower that forces air through a special plastic tray, where it obtains an electric charge. The air then moves under pressure through a special artificial fabric where the charge is increased.

Material is shoveled into the concentrator through a large screen that automatically classifies the material, letting only gravel less than half-an-inch in diameter into the concentrator. The material then works its way down through the recovery tray.

Gold is non-magnetic, but it has an affinity for an electrostatic charge, and is attracted to the special cloth that lines the recovery tray. The concentrator also works like a regular dry washer and traps the gold behind riffles.

Prospectors have been able to save even very fine pieces of gold with this machine.

Dry washing goes back to the earliest days of working the placers. Where there is no water to separate the gold from the other materials miners have devised several methods utilizing the flow of air to concentrate materials.

In the past most dry concentration was slow and inefficient. Even today most dry washers will have trouble recovering gold after the top layer of dry sand has been removed and the moist sand and gravel reached. Always make it a practice to run your material through your dry washer more than once.

One of the earliest methods of dry washing was known as winnowing. In winnowing, the coarse gravels are screened out and thrown away. Then the fines are placed on a blanket. The blanket is picked up by the corners and the fines tossed into the air in a strong wind. The lighter material is carried off by the wind and the heavier minerals fall back into the blanket. The weave of the blanket also helps to trap the flour gold.

Another method is to dry pan the gravels, but unless you are very experienced one could easily allow the valuable material to escape.

Working with a Dry Washer.

Another popular method of working dry placers is with a more simple type bellows dry washer. The gravels are shoveled onto a screen with a hopper underneath. The larger coarse gravels (normally a half-inch or more) are separated from the finer material dropping off the lower end of the screen, while the smaller material falls into the hopper. The smaller material is funneled down onto the riffle tray. The material flows down over the tray passing over the riffles where the gold is trapped. The flow of the material is aided by air pushed upwards by the bellows. The bellows can be operated by hand. A small gasoline engine can also be used to power the dry washer.

One of the latest and more popular machines on the market today is a battery powered dry washer. It can be operated by a small (motorcycle battery) that weighs very little and processes nearly a cubic yard per hour as illustrated. These lightweight new mini dry washers are ideal as they do not require fuel and can be recharged quickly.

Tools

White Adhesive Tape

A roll of white adhesive is a must. No, it's not for doctoring. It's for marking your ore samples. Whenever you locate a vein that you feel might contain values and you think should be assayed, use the tape to mark the location you got it from. God only knows how many pieces of rich ore I have seen that no one knows where it came from.

Write the date and the exact location where you found it on a piece of the tape and stick it on each piece of ore you bring in from the field as a sample for assaying.

The Shovel

You'll need a good shovel to dig up the dirt to put into your pan. Take your choice, long handled or short. The long handled shovel is easier on the back; the short handled one is easier to carry. You also should have a small hand garden trowel, for the hard to get at spots.

Tweezers

You will need a pair of the pointed jeweler's tweezers to pick the tiny flecks of gold from your pan.

Small Bottle

Find a small bottle or vial of clear glass or plastic to hold your colors.

Magnifying Glass

Any small magnifying glass that you can carry in your pocket will do. For home study, the magnifying glass attached to a flashlight is the best.

Knife

A plain hunting knife will do. Use this for digging, prying, and scraping.

Brush

A small paint brush can be used for cleaning out cracks and dusting crevices which are hiding gold, hopefully.

Bucket

Any regular household plastic bucket will suffice. The size will depend on how much you will want to carry.

Compass

Pick up a good compass before you go, it may save your life. Hundreds of stories are told of people losing their lives wandering aimlessly only a few miles from a main highway. Select a prominent landmark and note its direction from your campsite. Note also what direction the nearest main road lies.

Prospector's Hammer

You may want to invest in a prospector's hammer, which is used to split rocks to see if they contain any valuable minerals. You can also use the hammer end to pry with. It is pointed on one end and flat headed on the other. Buy a good one, otherwise the point on the cheaper ones will flatten out after very little use.

These are the basic tools you should have to start prospecting. As you go on in your golden quest, you will want to acquire more sophisticated equipment such as a sluice box, dry washer, dredge, concentrator, or metal detector.

Metal Detector

Not a requirement, but if you own a metal detector you should try a little nugget shooting in the dry washes. Here's the way you do it.

Pick a wash in one of the regions listed in this book. You're always better off in an area that you know has gold. Use the mineral setting to locate the black sand deposits and clean it off down to bedrock, if you can. Now put your detector back on metal and set it as fine as possible. Pass your detector over the area very slowly and watch your meter needle carefully. If you have headphones use them too. Check out every indication you receive. Some prospectors have had real good luck using this method of nugget shooting. See the chapter on Electronic Prospecting.

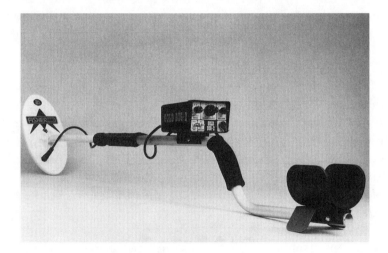

Fisher's Gold Bug Metal Detector.

Snake Bite Kit

You shouldn't enter upon a prospecting trip without bringing a snake bite kit along for protection. I know of several prospectors who owe their lives to the time given them by a snake bit kit. I've never been bit, but I've come close.

One hot summer day when working in an area south of the Turtle Mountains, I found myself running low on water. I decided to go to the Colorado River to replenish my supply.

I made my way to Highway 95 which runs along- side the river for about forty miles after it leaves Blythe on it's way to Needles. After I hit 95, I followed it for a few miles to a spot that looked pretty close to the river.

I parked my Bronco and took a couple of water cans and headed for the water. The brush gets pretty thick as you get near the river and I had to raise my foot pretty high to push it down to get through. Well, I was right smack dab in the middle of this brush when I ran into a four foot rattlesnake. I almost stepped on him as I was pressing down the brush with my foot. For a moment time seem to stand still as I tried to stop my foot from coming down on his back. That snake looked at me as if I was crazy. Then we both took off in opposite directions. If I live to a hundred and five I'll never forget the look on that snake's face. Some of the brush must have hit and scared it, for the snake to take off fast.

When people get bit it's mostly on the arms or hands. Be careful when you're climbing and don't stick your hands in holes you want to search without probing it with a long stick first.

The Vac Pac (Dry Crevis Vacuum)

Another new item for the prospector is the Vac Pac. This backpack machine can be used to vacuum crevices in both dry and wet areas, but it is more effective in dry areas. The material from crevices and cracks are vacuumed into a holding bucket, similar to a shop vacuum. It is powered by a small two-cycle engine that will run all day on a quart of gas, weighs about fifteen pounds, and is equipped with a six-foot-long suction hose.

I have found this tool very effective while using it in the cleaning of dry crevices and cracks that would normally be very difficult to clean.

The most effective use with this type of machine is to look for crevices that are not easily visible, because those that are easily found have generally been cleaned out.

The Vac-Pac. (Courtesy of Keene Engineering)

Electronic Prospecting

Introduction

The most exciting new development in gold hunting is electronic prospecting or nugget shooting, as it is better known. I wanted to give you the best information available and though I have done some nugget shooting, I am by no means an expert. I have asked James (Jimmy Sierra) Normandi, who qualifies an as an expert with any type of metal detector to help with this chapter. He has found many treasures both here and in other countries and has nugget hunted successfully all over as well.

He is the author of several books on metal detecting and has allowed us to use excerpts on finding gold nuggets. He has also helped design many of the outstanding metal detectors manufactured by White's Electronics.

WHICH DETECTOR IS BEST FOR GOLD PROSPECTING ?

"There are basically two types of detectors which can be used for gold prospecting: The first is a multipurpose unit, or one which was designed to be used for various purposes such as coin hunting, relic hunting or gold prospecting, merely by changing the settings or manner in which the detector is used. The second is a detector which is designed particularly for gold prospecting. The multipurpose detector has been around a long time and if the right one is chosen, can produce gold in most conditions. The second type has become very popular in recent years and is the unit of choice for the serious prospector. Which detector you choose for gold prospecting should be determined by how often you intend to use it for that purpose. In other words, how serious you intend to be about gold hunting. Obviously, if you intend to use your unit for many purposes, the multipurpose unit is best for you. If gold is your prime interest, the specialized unit will be the best choice.

White's Goldmaster 4 Metal Detector.

PROSPECTING EQUIPMENT

Now that you have chosen your new prospecting detector, or perhaps your multipurpose unit will do the job, you must gather together some important "tools of the trade."

HEADPHONES

A very important accessory and one which should always be included is a good set of headphones. You don't have to spend a fortune for headphones, but you should pick a pair which feel comfortable on your head and which you could wear for long periods of time without discomfort.

TROWELS

The most common digging tool is the common trowel. These come in a variety of sizes and shapes and your dealer will give you a good choice, I am sure. If he doesn't have one you like, just visit the local nursery or hardware store. A stainless steel trowel is a good investment as it will not rust and will give you a lifetime of use. Some have a serrated edge to cut roots when you have to dig around the base of a tree.

MAGNETIC HOE

My favorite tool is the hoe style pick. It has a claw head on one side and a flat pick mattock head on the other. It is not as good for removing dirt from a hole as the trowel, but is very valuable if the soil is hard or rocky.

ROCK PICK-CHISEL CREVICER

If you are working bedrock crevices, this can be invaluable. It is pretty hard to break heavy bedrock with a mayhoe or trowel. This tool is heavy itself and should only be carried when you expect to work in non-decomposed bedrock. Decomposed rock will break apart more easily with light tools. A small crevice tool also comes in handy for pulling out those tiny pieces of gold.

DIGGING POUCH

Most prospectors carry some sort of pouch to put their digging equipment in as well as to carry home the assorted pieces of trash they accumulate There are a multitude of digging pouches available in every shape and material. Merely choose the one that suits you.

HOW DO I FIND THE GOLD NUGGET?

Alright, you have the right detector, a good set of headphones, something to dig with and a pouch to place the trash items you have collected. Now you think you have a gold nugget located. But where is it? It must be small, because it keeps moving around in the ground as you try to locate it. If it were larger you would surely see it and you could be on your way. This is where the skill will come in. Some hunters use a small plastic gold pan or they use a small plastic cup. Some will just trickle the soil on the top of the loop.

WHAT SHOULD I PUT THE NUGGET IN?

Finally, you need something to put the gold into. The most practical container I have come across is a plastic 35mm film canister. It has a large opening. I wasted much time looking for small pieces of gold which missed the opening of my gold vial before I discovered the film canister. In addition, stay away from glass containers. Gold, even small pieces, will break the bottom out of a glass vial in time. If you find a piece of gold larger than will fit into a film canister, you have my permission to put it into your digging pouch or pocket.

IS A HIP MOUNT KIT ESSENTIAL?

Most gold prospecting units today are compact and light enough to operate in the standard hand held configuration. That is, with the control box mounted directly on the rod which is connected to the loop. The entire unit is, thus, in one piece. Some of us find this heavier than we would like, particularly when swinging it all day long. There are usually alternative mounting options supplied with all brands of detectors. The most common is the hip or belt mount. In this configuration, the control box is mounted on a belt around the waist and only the arm piece connected to the loop is swung over the ground. Multipurpose detectors are usually more bulky and heavier and are more frequently adapted with hip mount kits to give more comfortable operation. Most of these kits are reasonably priced and are well worth the investment.

Well, we have our detector, understood its use and hopefully practiced with it for a while. We have packed our vehicle with all the necessary gear and supplies we need for our trip and have chosen a place to try our luck. I mentioned earlier that most of the detectors acceptable for prospecting are very similar in their controls and operation. The specific operating instructions should be acquired from the factory manual and the dealer you purchased the detector from. I told you that there were basically two types of detectors used. First, the all purpose discrimination only and some with a meter or screen to help identify discriminated targets.

The second type is the specialized prospecting detector. These can also come with manual ground balancing or automatic tracking ground balancing. Some of these can have a form of discrimination to eliminate iron trash. These usually have a higher frequency and more effective ground canceling controls.

Let us start with the first time I went prospecting with a metal detector. At the time, there were no detectors specialized for prospecting only. Oh, there were a few which had names given to them by the manufacturers which were made to indicate that they were to be used for prospecting. But, in reality, they were really what I have been referring to as multi-purpose detectors. They were originally designed for coin hunting and, because of their ability to cancel mineralized ground, found double use as prospecting tools. I would never attempt to discredit this gender of detector. They have always produced ample quantities of gold and in fact still do. In fact, most of the large nuggets I know of were found over the years with this type of detector both here and in Australia.

Fortunately, I went with my good friend and mentor in the field of prospecting, Jim Williams of Rancho Cordova, California.

Jim pointed out some likely spots where he had found pieces of gold on the earlier trips and turned me loose. No instructions, of course, as I had been detecting for years and he didn't feel I needed any special advice. In retrospect, I am sure he just wanted me to learn the hard way, like he had. I set the detector in the all metal (non-motion mode of operation) and the discriminator dial set to just reject nails. I set the sensitivity at a level where there were no false or spurious noises when I moved the loop over the ground while searching. With the threshold hum at a faint level and the volume control on the headphones set to give a strong, but not ear shattering response to a target and the detector ground balanced, I was ready to start hunting. I was using a four inch coil on my detector as Jim had warned me that pieces of gold were small. I tried the tops of ridges, the steep banks, gullies, everywhere I thought a nugget might be hiding. I ground balanced the detector each time the ground started to get louder or softer. Ground balancing is essential.

I searched and searched until lunch time and had not found anything except for a few large lead rifle slugs. I could hear Jim yell every once in a while that he had found another piece. I had worked faster and faster hoping to get a piece before lunch. No such luck. What was I doing wrong? I had decided earlier that he had cleaned the place out and was letting me work the old areas while working the virgin territory himself but I asked him anyway. He answered straight away. "You're moving too fast . . . take your time . . . the targets are small . . . real small and they don't sound like coins . . . slow down your swing, almost crawl across the ground. Remember you are listening for a faint increase in the threshold hum. It will sound like a coin but much fainter."

After lunch, using his advise, my luck changed and I found my first small piece of gold.

If there is no discriminator or target identifier on the unit you are using you must dig all the targets if you want all the gold. After a while some prospectors say they can tell the difference between iron and non-iron by the sound. Nuggets seem to have a sharper peak and softer sound, iron targets seem to have a flatter or broader peak and sound harsher. And of course, the telltale double beep of a nail laying straight out is a clue for everyone using a non-discriminating detector for either coin hunting or prospecting. Tracing the size of the target is also a clue, but some nuggets can be awfully large and you wouldn't want to walk away from a big one. In this non-motion, all metal mode, you can also try the trick of seeing how large an area of the loop is sensitive to the target. For example, a non-iron target is usually detected only within the diameter (an area no wider than the loop), while an iron target is usually detected well beyond the edges of the loop. If you have no discriminator, learn to interpret targets; if you have one, learn its limitations. When in doubt, dig!

I mentioned that I had not attempted to use the discriminating capability of my unit in the excitement of my first find. Had I done it, I would still have had to dig the target because it was lead. If attempting to discriminate, the electronic prospector must dig all targets made of lead, brass, copper, aluminum and silver as they are all potentially able to be a piece of gold. Iron is the only type of trash one can chance to ignore. I have also mentioned, while describing different detectors, that no discriminator is infallible. The size of the target, the depth of the target and the degree of mineralization in the ground can all confuse even the best discriminator. In this particular location, the discriminators worked with pre-dictable dependability. The ground was modest and a little practice made the identification of iron pretty accurate. One has to weigh the value of leaving some small pieces of gold behind in this instance against digging a barrel full of nails and trash. I think most would agree that if the ground is too mineralized, the toss should go for digging everything. To find out if you can depend upon the discriminator, just use a few test nuggets in the ground.

I worked on top of the ridges and mounds where the winter and spring rains had washed some of the overburden off. I worked the banks which the water runoff had eroded. I worked the places where the bedrock was crumbly and you could see the cracks and crevices. All of these places produced gold. I noticed that I got pieces hidden under the limbs of bushes which others had ignored. This is the advantage of using a small loop. After the trip I felt that I had came back a little more of an expert.

It was only a matter of time after the modern Gold Rush started in Australia in the early 1980s before we would see metal detectors marketed for gold prospecting exclusively. They had the necessary features and capabilities and with time acquired names applied by marketing departments to enhance their sales. Some were better than others, but all found gold.

Little by little, certain features were changed and enhanced. Each bringing us a little better performance. Loops were developed to find smaller targets, to detect targets deeper, and to scan larger areas. Discriminators were modified for improved target identification. Operating frequencies were changed to achieve improved sensitivity to gold in mineralized ground. Thus, a new age was born, detectors designed especially for the gold market. The metal detector industry would never be the same.

All these gold detectors seem to share common traits: higher transmitting frequencies than multipurpose models, extensive ground balance capabilities, and steps to avoid overload in highly mineralized ground. It wasn't long before every manufacturer had their own favorite entry into this growing field.

Therefore it was soon realized by most manufacturers that higher transmitting frequencies saw smaller targets, and with gold areas being worked harder and harder, every target, no manner how small, was fair game. Of course, frequency isn't everything and the detector must fulfill all of the earlier mentioned qualities. Most of the entries in the market utilize manual ground canceling techniques, however there are some auto tracking units available. There are advantages to both styles. The choice is yours.

WHAT ABOUT HOT ROCKS?

This is about the nastiest word an electronic prospector can think of and one which can mean something different to almost everyone. I know there are technical definitions of hot rocks which I could conjure up but which wouldn't really do much to solve the problems they cause. I will try to put the whole issue into perspective and attempt to take away some of the fear of their presence.

The common denominator of all of these is the fact that they all make a noise when the detector loop is passed over them, thus misleading the operator into thinking that they are metal targets. I prefer to describe them as small or large concentrations of mineralization, usually in rock form, hotter than the surrounding ground in which they are found. By "hotter", I mean more heavily mineralized.

The thing you have to overcome in learning to deal with hot rocks is to put aside any fear you might have of them and to forget the idea that you must eliminate them. What you must do is learn to identify them. That is, you must be good at telling the difference between a hot rock and a real metal target. I would be suspicious of any detector that never heard a hot rock under any circumstances. A particular rock can be considered a hot rock in one area and not be one in another area. By now, you should be getting the point; a hot rock is considered hot depending upon its relationship to the ground it is found in. The greater the degree of difference in mineralization, the "hotter" the rock. Therefore, the fact that the rock makes a noise is due to the change in mineralization. Some hot rocks are so mineralized, that they not only give a metal like signal, but they can overload the audio of the detector and neutralize the effectiveness of the loop. In other words, they kill the detector's ability to detect any target.

Some of these hot rocks are on the surface of the ground and are much easier to identify. Some are deeper in the ground and some are as small as BB's. Since they exist partly due to their relationship with the surrounding ground, they present a somewhat different problem everywhere you encounter them. Therefore, there are many more hot rocks than you hear at any location. Some are too deep and some too small and some not mineralized enough in relationship to the ground. Thus, you will hear some and not hear others. You can obviously ignore the ones you do not hear.

Always tune or ground balance your detector to the general matrix of the ground. That is, to the average ground you are working in. Remember, the bulk of the gold nuggets you will retrieve will be found in the general matrix, and not necessarily under a hot rock. Now with the detector balanced, start to search. If you are going to have a problem with hot rocks, you will know about it in a short time, for you will hear noises you cannot seem to isolate. If you have a signal, that you can't seem to find because it moves around, be persistent. Isolate it. You must decide whether or not you are going to be bothered by hot rocks early on or you will be walking away from possible gold targets.

A few facts to think about: Very large hot rocks tend to give a sort of overshoot sound, like a "boingboing" with a sort of void in the middle, as the loop approaches and leaves the target. These are the easiest to isolate as they are usually on top of the ground and large. Just move them or walk around them. The same kind of rock, if found on top of the ground, will appear under the ground as well. If they are deep enough, you won't hear them at all. Hot rocks lose their bang very rapidly as they get farther from the loop. Metal targets get gradually softer as they get farther from the loop. Smaller hot rocks are obviously harder to find. They sound more like targets as they don't give the overshoot or "boing" sound. The little red ones are the worst. The best advice I can give you is that they tend to have a broader peak sound; not as sharp a peak as the "zip-zip" of a good nugget target. If this sounds awfully confusing, I don't blame you. It is until you experience it yourself.

Since all hot rocks are a different size and quality, you might have to balance a few more till you get the right amount of control. If you have to go too far off of the original ground balance to smooth out the hot rocks, the ground will start giving you a signal. This can obscure the good targets and could be worse than trying to adjust the ground control to ignore the hot rocks. Notice I said "ignore". This may be what you will have to do rather than adjust your detector to do it. That is, you may opt to train your ear to differentiate the different sound of a hot rock from the peaked zip of a nugget. You will learn in time which system is best for the particular area you are hunting.

Some prospectors who work with multi-purpose detectors utilize the rule that hot rocks that are detected on the all-metal mode, will not be detected on the discriminate mode and vice versa. Therefore, because prospecting is done in the all-metal mode, switching to the discriminate mode momentarily while passing over the target with the loop could identify a hot rock. Thus, a hot rock which sounds off on all-metal, will go blank on discriminate. The only weakness in this test, is that a small piece of gold in mineralized ground could also cause the sound to go blank, as it was not a good enough signal to react. It works well in moderate ground and for larger than grain size nuggets.

PUT IT IN THE SACK AND GO HOME!

Well, you bought your detector, stayed awake for the long drive to the gold fields, fought the mosquitoes, snakes, bears and hot rocks and finally are sure you have located a nugget. Now you must get it into your film canister.

The first and oldest method is merely to grab a handful of dirt and wave it over the loop. When your handful makes a sound, open your hand and look for the target. This works fine if the target is large and the loop is not so sensitive that it actually can pick up the salt in your body. The high frequency instruments are notorious for this and particularly White's Goldmaster II which operates at 50 KHZ. With these units, you should test the palm of your hand first. If the detector picks it up with a positive signal, then try your fingers. If this works, you can take pinches of dirt instead of a handful. As I said, this method works best when you are fairly sure you have a larger target.

The second method is called the sprinkle method. This is where the handful of dirt which is suspected of containing the nugget is sprinkled slowly in a stream on the TOP of the loop. If you are using this method, be sure that the loop is flat (horizontal) on the ground so that the nugget does not slide off of the loop back onto the ground.

Even a small flake of gold will stay when it lands on the loop. When the piece of gold hits the loop, you can hear the signal it causes. Sprinkle the soil a little at a time and tip the tested soil off of the loop before sprinkling a little more. I forgot to mention that the detector is obviously left on during this procedure and preferably with headphones on as well. This will work with both small and larger nuggets as they will both sound off when they bounce on the loop. A variation of this is merely to take handfuls of dirt progressively as you check the hole to see when the target disappears from the ground. When you are sure that the target is in your hand, just dump the dirt into your pouch. After the day's searching, take all the accumulated dirt and throw it into a pan and pan out the nuggets.

The third method is the one I prefer in the gritty or soft soil of the mountain areas. In this method the dirt is scooped into a plastic gold pan a small amount at a time. The pan is shaken to move the gold to the bottom; remember the density of gold will make it drop to the bottom through gravity. Then the pan is passed over the loop to ascertain whether or not the target is in it. If no signal is heard, test the pile to see if the target is still there and then toss the soil in the pan aside.

Notice I said to check the pile again first. The nugget could be small and not worked its way down to the bottom of the pan. If it is still in the pile you are alright. Take another scoop and continue the procedure. When you finally have the signal in the pan, remove some of the dirt to one side of the pan and check both piles. Keep this up till you have the pile small enough to blow the overburden off and leave the piece of gold exposed. This process is sometimes done on a rock if no pan is available. Just add dirt and separate into two piles progressively. I said I prefer this method, but I developed a special pan to make the process go more smoothly and efficiently. It is rectangular with a beveled shovel side and three raised edges.

It can be used as a shovel to scoop the dirt from the pile and even to dig a small depression on shallower nuggets. A small pocket or trap in the far end of the tray is helpful in trapping the piece of gold when the tray is shaken. The tray is passed over the loop as above and progressively soil is wiped off of the tray till the target is in the trap or at least near it. The dirt is then blown off of the piece of gold. Be careful, in areas where very tiny subgrain nuggets are found, you can actually blow the nugget out of the tray. This tray is called the Sierra Gold Tray and sells for $5.95 at most dealers. This works fine even when the soil is heavy. If the soil is muddy, you will probably have to use the pinch method and just put the collected target and dirt aside in your pouch to separate later.

Look carefully, it will be there. Put your nugget into your container, pat yourself on the back and shout EUREKA!" (excerpted from *Finding Gold Nuggets with a Metal Detector*)

5. How to Stake a Claim

If, by chance, you should strike El Dorado and locate a rich deposit of gold, you will need to know how to claim it for your own. Remember that the first men involved in writing California law were either miners or men connected with the Gold Rush in some way. Men like Hearst, Armour, and Stanford, whom we associate with newspapers, meat packing, and universities, began their fortunes in the gold fields. It was these same men who helped draft California's laws.

The state was dependent on the gold mining industry, and its land laws still favor the miner. If you own your home, you probably are aware that you do not always get mineral rights with your title. Mineral rights have to be claimed and proved if contested. Mineral rights belong to the locator.

If you locate a deposit you feel is worth developing, there are some basic things you can do to protect your discovery. First, as you know, there are two types of gold mines: placer and lode. Each has its own set of rules and regulations.

A placer claim may consist of as much as twenty acres for each person signing the location notice. Placer gold, again, is free gold found in gravels and alluvial deposits. You must place a Notice of Location on a post, tree, rock in place, or on a rock monument you build, showing the name of the claim, who is locating it, the date, and the amount of area claimed. You must mark the boundaries of your claim so that it may be easily traced. You must also identify the location of your claim by reference to some local landmark or natural object (such as a stream or rock formation) or a permanent monument. Finally, you must file a copy of Location Notice with the local county recorder within ninety days of the date of location.

142

A lode claim uses a different procedure. Lode gold, again, is gold in a vein, which must be mined and separated from its mother rock. The claim may consist of as much as 1500 feet along the sidelines of the vein, and 300 feet on each side of the middle of the vein. Within 90 days of the location of any lode mining claim, you must place a post or stone monument at each corner of the claim. The posts must be at least four inches in diameter, and the stone monuments must be at least eighteen inches high. A Notice of Location form must be posted on the claim, and a lode Location Notice filed with the county recorder and the state office of the Bureau of Land Management within 90 days.

This section is not intended to be a complete thesis on all the rules and regulations regarding mining claims, but it will help to protect you in the initial phases should you make a rich discovery. For more details, I recommend obtaining a copy of the *Legal Guide for California Prospectors and Miners, Special Publication 40*, put out by the State of California Department of Mines and Geology and *Stake Your Claim: How to Find Gold and Stake a Mining Claim* by Mark Silva.

LODE MINING CLAIM LOCATION NOTICE

Notice is hereby given that the undersigned have this _____ day of _____, 19____

located a lode mining claim on public (surveyed) (unsurveyed) lands in_____

Mining District, County of _____, State of California.

1. The name of this claim is _____. It is situated in:

NE¼ ☐	NW¼ ☐	SW¼ ☐	SE¼ ☐	Sec. _____	T. _____	R. _____	Mer. _____
NE¼ ☐	NW¼ ☐	SW¼ ☐	SE¼ ☐	Sec. _____	T. _____	R. _____	Mer. _____
NE¼ ☐	NW¼ ☐	SW¼ ☐	SE¼ ☐	Sec. _____	T. _____	R. _____	Mer. _____
NE¼ ☐	NW¼ ☐	SW¼ ☐	SE¼ ☐	Sec. _____	T. _____	R. _____	Mer. _____

2. The locator or locators of this claim are:

Name(s)	Current Mailing or Residence Address
_____	_____
_____	_____
_____	_____
_____	_____

3. The number of linear feet claimed in length along the course of the vein each way from the point of discovery is _____
    (not to exceed 1500 feet)
    in a _____ direction, and _____ feet in a _____ direction. The width on
    each side of the center of the claim is _____ feet.
    (not to exceed 300 feet)

4. The claim, described by reference to some natural object or permanent monument as will identify the claim located, is
    as follows: _____
    _____
    _____

5. This claim covers, among other things, all dips, variations, spurs, angles and all veins, ledges, and other valuable deposits
    within the lines of this claim, together with all water and timber and any other rights appurtenant, as allowed by the laws of
    this State and/or the United States.

Dated: _____, 19____   Signature(s) _____
_____

NOTICE IS HEREBY GIVEN by the undersigned locator(s) that in accordance with the requirements of California Public Resources
Code:

1. The above notice of location is a true copy of said notice; and is hereby incorporated by reference herein and made a part hereof.

2. The locator(s), within the prescribed time, as required by law, have defined the boundaries of this claim by erecting at each
    corner of the claim and at the center of each end line, or nearest accessible points thereof, a conspicuous and substantial
    monument; and each corner monument so erected bears or contains markings sufficient to appropriately designate the
    corner of the mining claim to which it pertains and the name of the claim. The date of marking is: _____;
    and the description of monuments is: _____
    _____

3. The United States survey within which all or any part of the claim is located is:
    Section _____, Township _____, Range _____, _____Meridian.

Dated: _____, 19____   Signature(s) _____
_____

CLAIMS LOCATED AFTER OCTOBER 21, 1976, MUST BE RECORDED WITH THE BUREAU OF LAND MANAGEMENT **WITHIN 90
DAYS AFTER DATE OF LOCATION.**

CSO 3800-2
6/79

(SEE REVERSE SIDE)

WOLCOTTS FORM 1134—LODE MINING CLAIM LOCATION NOTICE—Rev. 3-80   (price class 3)

Sample of Lode Mining Claim Location Notice.

PLACER MINING CLAIM LOCATION NOTICE

TO WHOM IT MAY CONCERN: Please take notice that:

1. The name of this claim is _____, a placer mining claim.

2. This claim is situated in:

NE¼ ☐	NW¼ ☐	SW¼ ☐	SE¼ ☐	Sec. _____T. _____R. _____Mer. _____
NE¼ ☐	NW¼ ☐	SW¼ ☐	SE¼ ☐	Sec. _____T. _____R. _____Mer. _____
NE¼ ☐	NW¼ ☐	SW¼ ☐	SE¼ ☐	Sec. _____T. _____R. _____Mer. _____
NE¼ ☐	NW¼ ☐	SW¼ ☐	SE¼ ☐	Sec. _____T. _____R. _____Mer. _____

   in the _____ Mining District, County of _____, State of California.

   The acreage claimed is _____ acres.

3. The date of this location is the _____ day of _____, 19___ on which date the notice of location was posted on the claim.

4. The locator or locators of this claim are:

Name(s)	Current Mailing or Residence Address
_____	_____
_____	_____
_____	_____
_____	_____
_____	_____
_____	_____
_____	_____

5. If claim cannot be described by quarter-section, the boundaries of the claims and the land taken are described as follows:

   Commencing at the discovery monument where this notice is posted, thence _____ to the _____ corner which is the point of the beginning to describe the boundaries, (direction)

   thence _____ _____ feet to the _____ corner,
           (direction)
   thence _____ _____ feet to the _____ corner,
           (direction)
   thence _____ _____ feet to the _____ corner,
           (direction)
   thence _____ _____ feet to the point of beginning.
           (direction)

6. The discovery monument is situated at the point of discovery about _____ (distance from natural object or permanent monument and give direction as accurately as possible, to identify the claim located)

SIGNATURE(S)

_____   _____
_____   _____
_____   _____

CLAIMS LOCATED AFTER OCTOBER 21, 1976, MUST BE RECORDED WITH THE BUREAU OF LAND MANAGEMENT **WITHIN 90 DAYS AFTER DATE OF LOCATION.**

CSO 3800-1
6/79

WOLCOTTS FORM 1130—PLACER MINING CLAIM LOCATION NOTICE—Rev. 3-80

Sample of a Placer Mining Claim Location Notice.

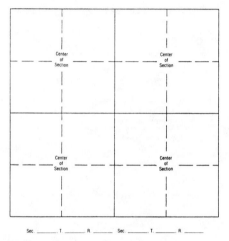

This form has been designed through the courtesy of the U.S. Department of the Interior, Bureau of Land Management, to assist you in recording your mining claim.

In accordance with Section 314 of the Act of October 21, 1976, as amended, Public Law 94-579 (90 Stat. 2743), the Federal Land Policy and Management Act of 1976, all unpatented lode or placer mining claims or mill or tunnel site claims on public lands of the United States in the State of California shall be recorded with the Bureau of Land Management, California State Office, Federal Office Building, Room E-2841, 2800 Cottage Way, Sacramento, California 95825. Copies of the regulations may be obtained from this office.

FILE ORIGINAL WITH COUNTY RECORDER
MAIL DUPLICATE COPY TO:
USDI BUREAU OF LAND MANAGEMENT
STATE OFFICE
Federal Office Building
2800 Cottage Way E-2841
Sacramento, California 95825

SHOW SITE OF CLAIM

DIAGRAM CONTAINS FOUR COMPLETE SECTIONS

Sec _____ , T _____ , R _____   Sec _____ , T _____ , R _____

Any person who willfully makes a false statement with respect to any mining claim on the posted location notice or on the recorded notice shall be deemed guilty of a misdemeanor, and upon conviction shall be punished by a fine not exceeding one hundred dollars ($100) or by imprisonment in the county jail not exceeding six months, or by both such fine and imprisonment. (Public Resources Code of California. Sec. 2315).

Sec _____ , T _____ , R _____   Sec _____ , T _____ , R _____

CALIFORNIA LAWS FOR MINES AND MINING
from California Public Resources Code
Division 2, Chapter 4
MANNER OF LOCATING MINING CLAIMS, TUNNEL RIGHTS AND MILL SITES

§ 2303. Location of placer claims; manner of location; location by legal subdivision

The location of a placer claim shall be made in the following manner:

(a) By erecting at the point of discovery thereon a conspicuous and substantial monument, and by posting in or on the monument, a notice of location containing the name of the

claim, the name, current mailing address or current residence address of the locator or locators, the date of posting such notice, the number of feet or acreage claimed, and such a description of the claim by reference to some natural object or permanent monument as will identify the claim located.

(b) By marking the boundaries so that they may be readily traced and by erecting at each corner of the claim, or at the nearest accessible points thereto, a conspicuous and substantial monument. Each corner monument shall bear or contain markings sufficient to appropriately designate the corner of the mining claim to which it pertains and the name of the claim.

Where the United States survey has been extended over the land embraced in the location, however, the claim may be taken by legal subdivisions and no other reference than those of such survey shall be required, and the boundaries of a claim so located and described need not be staked or monumented. The description by legal subdivisions shall be deemed the equivalent of marking.

(Stats. 1939, c. 93, p. 1080, § 2302. Amended by Stats. 1970, c. 90, p. 109, § 3.)

§ 2312. Location of nonmineral land as millsite; manner of location

The proprietor of a vein or lode claim or mine, the proprietor of a placer claim, or the owner of a quartz mill or reduction works, or any person qualified by the laws of the United States may locate not more than five acres of nonmineral land as a millsite. The location shall be made and the claim boundaries marked in the same manner as required by Section 2303 for locating placer claims, except that the monument in or on which the notice of location is posted may be erected anywhere within the claim, and location work is not required.

(Stats. 1939, c. 93, p. 1083, § 2312. Amended by Stats. 1970, c. 90, p. 111, § 9.)

Reverse side of the Placer Mining Claim Location Notice.

146

6. GLOSSARY

ALLOY - A solid solution of two or more minerals.

ALLUVIAL - Loose gravel, soil, or mud, deposited by water.

AMALGAM - Normally a physical alloy of mercury with gold or silver.

ARRASTRE - A circle of stones where ore was crushed during the early days of gold mining; a primitive but effective method of separating gold from quartz.

ASSAY - To evaluate the quantity and quality of the minerals in an ore.

AURIFEROUS - Containing gold or gold bearing.

BAR - A name given to the sandbars and rock and gravel bars found in rivers, primarily when they're gold-bearing.

BENCHES - All kinds of rock or gravels shaped like terraces or steps. Bench placers are found on the canyon walls above the present streambeds.

BIRD'S-EYE PORPHYRY - The name given to intrusive igneous rocks by local miners.

BLACK SAND - These are usually made up of magnetite, tourmaline, ilmenite, chromite, and cassiterite. They are found in rivers, beaches, sluice boxes, and pans. Black sand will usually be found with gold, but gold is not always found with black sand.

BURIED CHANNEL - Places where a stream has been covered by lava, mud flows, ash falls, landslide matter, gravel, or lake deposits.

COLOR - Any amount of gold found in a prospector's pan after a sample of dirt has been panned.

DETRITAL GOLD - Loose gold resulting directly from disintegration.

DIGGINGS - A claim or place being worked.

DIORITE - A granular, crystalline, igneous rock in which gold sometimes occurs.

DISINTEGRATION - To undergo a change in composition by decomposing into constituent elements, parts or small particles.

DREDGING - A method of vacuuming gold bearing gravels from river or stream bottoms.

DRIFT - A horizontal tunnel following a vein or gold bearing gravels.

DRY WASHER - A machine which separates gold from gravels by the flow of forced air.

ELOVIAL PLACERS - Hillside placer deposits between residual and stream deposits.

EOLIAN PLACERS - Placers borne, deposited, produced or eroded by wind.

FLOAT - Loose pieces of ore broken off a vein outcropping. Prospectors will follow the float to its source to locate a lode.

GANGUE MATERIALS - The worthless rock or vein matter in which valuable metals or minerals occur.

GLORY HOLE - A small but very rich deposit of gold ore.

GRAVEL BENCHES - Gravel deposits left on canyon walls through stream erosion.

GULCH - A small canyon or ravine.

HARDROCK MINING - Another term for lode mining.

HEADFRAME - The support structure located at the entrance of a mine over a shaft. Used for hoisting.

HYDRAULIC MINING - A very destructive and now outlawed form of gold mining used in the Gold Rush. Giant hoses were used to force great streams of water onto canyon walls containing gold bearing gravels. The walls were washed away into sluice boxes, where the gold was then picked out.

IRON PYRITE - A common mineral consisting of iron disulfide which has a pale, brass yellow color and a brilliant metallic luster. Also called fool's gold.

LODE - A vein of gold mined either through a tunnel or a shaft.

MATRIX - The material in which the gold is found.

PLACER - Free occurring gold which is usually found in stream and river gravels.

POCKET - A rich deposit of gold occurring in a vein or in gravels.

POKE - A leather pouch used by old-time miners to hold their gold.

QUARTZ - A common mineral, consisting of silicon dioxide, that often contains gold or silver.

RESIDUAL PLACERS - Gold released from vein material and broken down by weathering.

RETORT - A device used to separate gold from mercury.

RICH FLOAT - Gold bearing rocks worked loose from a lode.

ROCKER - A device used by the early miners during the Gold Rush. This was a sluice box mounted on rockers with a hopper on the top to classify the material. Gravels were shoveled into the hopper; then water was poured on top, washing the gold bearing material down over the riffles while the hopper was rocked. The rocking helped the gold to settle.

SEDIMENTARY ROCK - Rock formed from mechanical, chemical or organic sediment. Also rock formed of fragments transported from their source and deposited elsewhere by water.

SCHIST - A crystalline rock which is easily split apart.

SLUICE BOX - A trough with obstructions to trap gold used in continuously moving water.

STAMP MILL - A machine used to crush ore.

SULFIDE - A compound of sulfur and any other metal.

TAILINGS - The material thrown out when ore is processed. The tailings from the early mines, where the miners were sometimes very careless, have produced significant amounts of gold and other valuable minerals.

TERRACE DEPOSITS - Gravel benches high on canyon walls.

TERTIARY - Belonging to or designating the geologic time, system of rocks, and sedimentary deposits of the first period of the Cenozoic era.

TOPOGRAPHY - The configuration of a surface, including its relief and position of its nature, matrix and features.

TRANSVERSE FAULT - The strike of a fault, normally across.

WALL - The rock on either side or a vein.

WINNOWED - Treated or exposed to a current of air so that waste matter is eliminated.

WIRE GOLD - Gold thinly laced through rock.

7. About the Author

James Klein was born in Beechgrove, Indiana, in 1932, and arrived in California at the age of 14. After attending Los Angeles City College and U.C.L.A., he went to work at the *Old Daily News*. He later moved to the *Los Angeles Mirror-News*, and then to the *Los Angeles Herald Examiner.*

During his years as a newspaperman, he began doing small parts in motion pictures and television. He now devotes his time to acting and prospecting. First introduced to gold prospecting as a young man by a friend, he caught gold fever almost at once. He is also partner in the K. & M. Mining Explorations Company, which is now developing three gold mining claims. When not acting, Jim, along with his sons, loves to spend time exploring the outdoors for new deposits. He often spends time traveling as a guest speaker or doing exhibitions on gold prospecting.

Notes